The Xbox 360
PocketGuide

Bart G. **Farkas**

All the Secrets of the Xbox 360, Pocket Sized.

**Peachpit
Press**

The Xbox 360 Pocket Guide
Bart G. Farkas

Peachpit Press
1249 Eighth Street
Berkeley, CA 94710
510/524-2178
800/283-9444
510/524-2221 (fax)

Find us on the Web at: www.peachpit.com
To report errors, please send a note to errata@peachpit.com

Peachpit Press is a division of Pearson Education

Editor: Clifford Colby
Production Editor: Connie Jeung-Mills
Compositor: WolfsonDesign
Indexer: Julie Bess
Cover design: Aren Howell
Cover photography: Aren Howell
Interior design: Kim Scott, with Maureen Forys

ISBN 13: 978-0-321-54495-7
ISBN 10: 0-321-54495-1

9 8 7 6 5 4 3 2 1

Printed and bound in the United States of America

For Cori

Acknowledgments

Special thanks to Cliff Colby, who worked so hard to get the book going and for finding so much of the hard-to-come-by art! I must also thank everyone at Peachpit who had a hand in producing, laying out, indexing, boxing, shipping, or otherwise handling this book. On the home front, I need to thank my wife, Cori, and my children—Derek, Adam, and Natasha—for their patience while I put the time in to write this. I also want to thank my father, Glen, and my mother, Lu, for their help in babysitting. Lastly, I need to thank Harry and Myrna Kruger, Lisa Pobran, and Kim Hilliard for their help.

About the Author

Bart G. Farkas is a full-time writer who lives in the shadow of the Canadian Rocky Mountains with his wife, three children, and three cats.

In his spare time, Bart is a scout leader and an active football official, working in various capacities at both the amateur and professional level.

Contents

Introduction

The Xbox 360 is arguably the king of the gaming consoles when it comes to raw power and functionality. Indeed, the Xbox 360 sales are brisk, and with the fall 2007 release of the flagship game Halo 3, Microsoft's gaming box is even more entrenched in our imaginations.

Even without Halo 3, however, the Xbox 360 is fully capable of becoming a centerpiece media appliance in our homes and businesses. With its ability to connect to Windows-based PCs and manage movies, photos, music, and all things gaming, the Xbox 360 has earned a spot in millions of homes around the world.

This book endeavors to be the first line of information for those entering the world of the Xbox 360 for the first time. Indeed, if you are getting a 360 for yourself, or your kids, or even as a holiday gift but you aren't entirely sure what it can do, then this is the book for you. Each chapter endeavors to explain a key aspect of Xbox gaming to you so that by the end of the book your knowledge of what the 360 can do is on par with savvy Xbox owners who have been a part of the culture for years.

Enjoy!

1

The Xbox 360

Back in the mist-shrouded first days of the new century, Microsoft announced that its role in the gaming world was about to move from a peripheral player that concentrated on a few key games to a central figure in the console-gaming realm. And indeed, in the fall of 2001—on November 15, 2001—the Microsoft Xbox arrived.

The Xbox promised incredible gaming power based on existing computing technology, and it certainly delivered. While not the dominant force in the market, the Xbox carved out a niche for itself, and four years later (almost to the day) the Xbox 360 arrived to take Microsoft's gaming dream to the next level.

The Xbox 360 is an incredibly powerful gaming machine with a great deal of flexibility built in to its components. The 360 can do everything from single-player gaming to online gaming (complete with headsets and video feeds) to acting as a shopping platform for electronic entertainment. And if that isn't enough, the 360 can also serve as a very competent media center that can manage all of your music, movies, games, and photos in one convenient and powerful box.

This pocket guide is designed to help you get going, from opening up the Xbox 360 packaging to taking advantage of each feature you want to use. Because we've broken the chapters up into nice bite-sized chunks of information, you can quickly read about the aspects of the 360 you wish to use and then delve into to making the most of your purchase.

A Brief History of the Xbox

The genesis of the Xbox probably goes back to the 1990s when console gaming started to rocket to the forefront of the digital entertainment market. Prior to the rise of consoles, PCs were the dominant force in gaming, largely because computers offered so much power and flexibility (and connectivity) not available to the low-cost consoles. In the '90s, however, the Sony PlayStation's huge success seems to have poked the sleeping bear known as Microsoft, and by late in the 1990s Mr. Gates's company was well into the planning phase of its new gaming machine.

According to the book *Opening the Xbox: Inside Microsoft's Plan to Unleash an Entertainment Revolution* by Dean Takahashi, the original name for the Xbox was to have been the DirectX-box. This name will make sense to those folks who know that Microsoft's DirectX software lets games take advantage of everything modern computers have to offer under the Microsoft Windows operating system. Ultimately, however, the name morphed into just the Xbox, and indeed, the *X* part of it even showed up on the top of the original Xbox as part of the design. The original Xbox sold for $299 U.S., and while it didn't outsell the competing consoles at the time (the GameCube and the PlayStation 2), spurred on by a game called Halo—which is exclusive to the Xbox—and by Microsoft's stubborn devotion to its console, the Xbox was able to find its place among the other consoles. The Xbox was aided by a few other successful and exclusive games and the burgeoning online gaming trend. The Xbox has an add-on capability called Xbox Live that allows players to play online, over the Internet, against players from all over the world. Most of all, the Xbox was easy to use, and as online gaming took off, so did the popularity of the Xbox.

Console Gaming

When we refer to *console gaming,* we are talking about games played on an independent machine that is apart from a computer. Examples of consoles include the Sony PlayStation, the Nintendo GameCube, the Sega Dreamcast, and their predecessors dating back nearly 30 years. Indeed, the original Pong game that Atari released to the home market is one of the first console games.

And if you think that Microsoft wasn't dedicated to the Xbox, then you should consider that in September 2005, Microsoft reported that it had absorbed a four *billon* dollar loss in selling the Xbox over the previous four years. This loss came largely from the costs of the hardware in the Xbox (which is basically a PC computer with a high-end video card) and the need to sell the Xbox at a low price to compete with Sony's and Nintendo's consoles.

In 2006 the Xbox 360 (**FIGURE 1.1**) hit the streets, and as one might expect, the newest Xbox is a bigger and better machine with a faster processor, larger hard drive, faster video card, wireless controllers, and a bevy of new features that immediately made it the technological king of the console market. The Xbox 360 is a fantastic gaming machine that also strives to be the multimedia centerpiece of the home, and its ongoing success appears guaranteed.

Figure 1.1
The Xbox 360, released in 2006.

The Guts and the Glory: What's Inside the Xbox 360

The Xbox 360 is the latest version of Microsoft's Xbox gaming system. This is pretty much what the average person knows about the Xbox 360. There are, however, some very impressive technological goodies inside this console that make it a real humdinger of a gaming machine. An important thing to note about the Xbox 360 is that it's basically a PC—that's right—a home computer! Microsoft with the original Xbox basically took a stripped-down home PC, added enough memory and a fast video card to make it a great game player, and put it in a box. While I admit that's a gross oversimplification, it's fundamentally true. The Xbox 360 is much more advanced, however, and uses a new processor that's you won't find in the average PC. But at its heart, it's still a PC that's tricked out to run games in high definition.

There are, as I write this, three basic versions of the Xbox 360 gaming console: The Xbox 360 Arcade, the Xbox 360, and the Xbox 360 Elite. Fundamentally, the only machine that has any differences in its guts is the Elite, so the following is a list of the key features of the Xbox 360, with a few notes on differences with the Arcade and Elite:

- 20 GB hard drive (no hard drive for Arcade; 120 GB hard drive for Elite).

- Standard video cable (included HDMI and Component HD cables for Elite).

- One-month trial of Xbox Live.

- Use as many as four wireless headsets and controllers simultaneously.

- 12X DVD drive (HD DVD drive is an accessory).

- 3.2 GHz triple-core PowerPC-based central processor.

- ATI Xenos dual-chip graphics processing unit (video card).

- 512 MB of 700 MHz RAM.

- All Xbox 360 games support 5.1 channel Dolby Digital surround sound, and the 360 includes a 32-bit processor for audio.

- All versions of the Xbox 360 support high-definition outputs; however, only the Xbox 360 Elite comes with the cabling necessary for HD out of the box.

- Only the Xbox 360 Elite is capable of HDMI output.

- Each Xbox 360 comes with one wireless controller.

- Three USB 2.0 slots available (a USB hub can be used to create more USB slots).

- Two memory card slots.

- Ethernet 10/100-Mbps connection.

note As of this writing there is also an Xbox 360 Halo 3 Edition console and an Xbox 360 Simpsons Movie console for sale, but these versions don't offer anything other than a different cosmetic covering and the inclusion of the Halo 3 game or the *Simpsons Movie* game.

High-Definition Multimedia Interface (HDMI)

HDMI is an audio/video connector that has become the state-of-the-art standard for computers and high-end gaming consoles. Basically HDMI is an all-in-one connector for sound and audio that helps to ensure the highest quality while also providing another check for digital rights management.

HDMI supports 8-channel digital audio as well as Dolby Digital, DTS, Dolby TrueHD, and DTS-HD Master Audio. Many computer monitors and other electronic multimedia products use the HDMI as the standard interface, and the fact that it's backward-compatible with most computer DVI (Digital Visual Interface) connectors makes it an excellent choice for products such as the Xbox 360.

Xbox 360 Arcade

Priced at $279, the Xbox 360 Arcade is the low-cost model in the Xbox 360 line. The main difference between the Arcade and the other models is that the Arcade lacks a hard drive (it does include a 256 memory module) and comes with a handful of games. While the lack of a hard drive may not seem terribly important when you consider that all games come on DVD and therefore don't require a hard drive, missing all the storage space limits many of the cool features the Xbox 360 offers. For example, a hard drive is the default location to store saved game data, but on the Xbox 360 Arcade you must use the included memory unit for this purpose. The hard drive also stores the large updates you download that allow you to play older Xbox games on the 360; and it is where demos, music videos, and movie trailers get stored when you download them off of the Xbox Live Marketplace. If any of these features interest you, play the extra cost and pick up an Xbox 360 with a hard drive; it'll save you a lot of grief.

Xbox 360

The Xbox 360 is the standard system and includes a wireless controller (**Figure 1.2**), a 20 GB hard drive, and a wired Xbox Live headset for your gaming pleasure. At $349, these features are reflected in the price, but for most users the extra $70 is worth what it buys. Unless you plan on storing heaps of music and home movies on your Xbox or you are going to be downloading a ton of online games, movie trailers, and game demos, the 20 GB hard drive should do the trick for you.

Figure 1.2
The Xbox 360 is the standard model and includes a wireless controller (the Arcade comes with one too).

Xbox 360 Elite

The Xbox 360 Elite is the most expensive of the three Xbox options, and it is up to you and your usage habits whether it's worth spending $449 for the Elite console (**Figure 1.3**). The most eye-popping features of the Elite are its 120 GB hard drive and a cool black finish, but it also comes with the HD Component and HDMI cables. Otherwise, it still includes a wired

Xbox Live headset and a black wireless controller. The main reason to buy the Xbox 360 Elite is if you plan on using your 360 as a media center in your home. If this is the case, then the extra hard drive space is likely to come in *very* handy as you route your multimedia through your Xbox.

Figure 1.3
The 360 Elite represents the costliest and best configured of the 360s.

What Makes the 360 So Great?

With all the talk and hype, you might well ask what makes the Xbox 360 so great? What makes it better than, say, the PlayStation 3 or Nintendo's Wii or GameCube? These questions are largely a matter of opinion, and so understand that opinion is what you are getting here; however, a few key aspects of the 360 make it superior to the other systems.

The games

First, the absolute most important aspect of any console system are the games available for it. Without an arsenal of killer games, even the most technologically jaw-dropping console is doomed to failure. Indeed, many pundits feel that a special game can drive the sales of a gaming unit, and it'd be hard to argue that this wasn't the case with Halo and the first Xbox consoles. Many (including myself) feel that Halo single-handedly saved the Xbox by driving gamers to buy the console solely so that they could play Halo.

The Xbox 360 now has many great games available for it, from Halo 1, 2, and now 3 (**Figure 1.4**) to nonstandard games such as Guitar Hero and Dance Dance Revolution. The Xbox 360's raw power has attracted makers of popular PC-based games to

Figure 1.4
Halo 3 is a killer game.

bring their games over to the Xbox, and since the Xbox 360 is largely backward-compatible with the games written for previous versions of the Xbox, the library of fun and entertaining games is significant. This fact alone makes the Xbox an attractive system.

The interface

The Xbox 360's interface—which is also known as Xbox Dashboard—(**FIGURE 1.5**) is another selling point. A graphically interesting and intuitive system allows users to log in to the Xbox Live Marketplace and download free game demos, music videos, music, movie trailers, and television shows.

Figure 1.5
The Xbox interface, called the Dashboard.

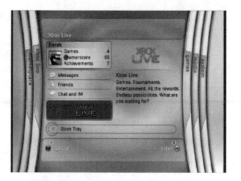

Users can also create their own gaming personas, which are forever saved (usually on the Xbox's hard drive) and which develop as you play games with your personas. And the basic Xbox 360 system allows gamers to stay in touch with one another and even keep track of their gaming achievements across all the various games they play. That gamers can chat with other gamers and meet up for online gaming gives the Xbox 360 a sort of soul that personalizes the gaming experience.

The tabs available in Xbox Dashboard are marked clearly on the screen (as shown in Figure 1.6), but it's worth mentioning briefly what each tab gives you (see the sidebar "Setting the Settings" for the System tab):

- **Marketplace.** While there is some overlap with the Media, Games, and Xbox Live tabs here, Marketplace is where you can go to purchase Microsoft Points and games and other multi-media content for your 360.

- **Xbox Live.** Here's where you can manage every aspect of your Xbox Live account.

- **Games.** This is where you create your gamer profile, manage Xbox Live Arcade issues, find new game demos, and even access the current game that's in the DVD drive of your Xbox 360.

- **Media.** The Media tab is where the gaming Xbox 360 meets the media center portions of the Xbox 360. Check out Chapter 8, "The Xbox 360 As a Media Center," for more details on this tab.

Setting the Settings

The Xbox Dashboard is the interface through which you communicate with your Xbox and Xbox Live. To tweak the key settings of your Xbox 360—from adjusting the display resolution, and choosing between a wireless and wired network to setting up a connection with a Windows-based PC—the one area in the Dashboard that you need to be familiar with is the System area.

To get to the System area, use the control stick on your controller to move to the System tab (**Figure 1.6**) and then get into the nitty-gritty of what needs to be done. The settings in this area are as follows:

- **Console Settings.** These are the settings for the display, audio, language, remote control, and other base pieces.

- **Family Settings.** This allows you to set limits on what your kids can play with and whom they can communicate with online.

- **Memory.** This is where you can go to copy saved games from your hard drive over to a memory unit or visa versa.

- **Network Settings.** Here you can adjust the network settings for wireless or wired networks and even the down-and-dirty network connections. That said, most networks connect to the Xbox automatically and easily.

- **Computers.** This allows you to set which computers your Xbox talks to.

- **Xbox Live Vision.** If you have one of these little cameras, use this area to set the brightness and black level of the camera as well as the focus.

- **Initial Setup.** This is there just in case you want to run through the initial setup procedure again at some point.

Figure 1.6
The System tab in the Xbox Dashboard gives you the ability to change the settings for most aspects of your Xbox 360.

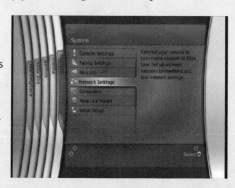

Online play

Perhaps the No. 1 reason that the Xbox and Xbox 360 have become so successful is the clever and seamless integration of online multiplayer gameplay into the 360 experience. With a high-speed Internet connection, players can go online and easily meet up with other players from around the world and play against (or with) one another for hours on end. The cost of this service is nominal, and with Microsoft making audio and video communication a simple part of many of the games, it allows the gamer to play while communicating directly with his or her friends (or foes). A great example of this is multi-player Call of Duty 3, a World War II-based game that involves squad-level combat. When playing online on Xbox Live, the player can talk with other members of his or her squad (with headsets like that shown in **FIGURE 1.7**), making it possible to communicate with each other during the battle, saying things like "He's behind the staircase. Watch out!"

Figure 1.7
A wired Xbox
Live headset.

The cooperative nature of online play—in many situations and across many genres of games—has made the Xbox Live portion of the Xbox 360 experience one of the most popular aspects of gaming on the Xbox and now the Xbox 360. Even if you think you are not the kind of person who would be interested in playing online against other players, it's still worth a try because, believe me, you may very well be surprised with how much fun it is.

The last important part of the online experience is the Xbox Live Marketplace, which allows you to shop for new and exciting games, music, and movies, all from the comfort of your living room sofa (or wherever your Xbox 360 is located). The enjoyment of having everything in one place and accessible by a wireless controller makes the appeal of the Xbox 360 easy to understand.

2

The 360: Out of the Box

Depending on the version of the Xbox 360 you purchase, the accessories that come with your machine vary considerably. This chapter takes a look at what comes with each particular Xbox 360 configuration, how you set up your 360, and how you navigate the Xbox 360 Dashboard. Fortunately, the Xbox 360s are mostly plug-and-play propositions, so you shouldn't be too challenged when setting up your system for the first time.

Inside the Box

Before we look at the 360's interface, let's see just what one receives when one purchases each of the three Xbox console configurations. The variations aren't significant on the surface, but the differences can affect what features are available to you for various games and activities.

The Xbox 360 Arcade console

The Arcade 360 lists for $279.99, and at its low price, it doesn't include some of the features and accessories that you will find in the more expensive Xbox 360 systems. The most important item lacking from the Arcade's feature list is a hard drive. Without a hard drive, it's not possible to update the Xbox Dashboard software on the 360, and therefore, you cannot update the Arcade to play original Xbox games on the 360.

If you want to hook up a hard drive, the Xbox 360 Hard Drive comes in two flavors, the 120 GB model, which sells for around $159.99, and the 20 GB model, which goes for $99.99. Clearly the larger hard drive is the better value dollar-for-dollar, but either will do the trick.

The Arcade does come with a 256 MB memory module, so you will be able to save games, info for your Xbox Live account, and a photo or two.

Here's the Xbox 260 Arcade items:

- Xbox 360 console.

- Standard AV cable.

- Wireless controller.

- Power cord and transformer.

- 256 MB memory module.

- Xbox Live Silver membership.

- Five Xbox Live Arcade games: Boom Boom Rocket, Feeding Frenzy, Luxor 2, Pac-Man Championship Edition, and UNO.

note Having a larger hard drive on your 360 means that you can download many more game demos, videos, movies, movie trailers, music, photos, and other digital content onto your Xbox 360.

The Xbox 360 console

The Xbox 360 console is the standard 360 and retails for $349.99.
This version of the 360 comes with
everything you need to get started,
play original Xbox games, and even
communicate and connect on Xbox
Live. If you can afford it, this console is
definitely the way to go, since adding
just the hard drive to a Arcade system
is ultimately more expensive.

The Xbox 360 console comes with the
following equipment:

- Xbox 360 console.

- Standard AV cable.

- Component AV cable (for high-definition
  televisions).

- Wireless controller.

- Power cord and transformer.

- Ethernet cable.

- 20 GB hard drive.

- Xbox Live wired headset.

- Xbox Live Silver membership (one-month trial
  Gold membership).

Halo 3 and Simpsons Movie special edition Xbox 360s

These are standard Xbox 360 systems dressed up with special packaging and come with a wireless controller and 20 GB hard drive. The Halo 3 Special Edition, for example, is decked out in Halo colors and art, although you can't really tell that in the black-and-white image below.

The Xbox 360 Elite console

Having recently purchased one myself, I can say without reservation that the Xbox 360 Elite is the most pimped out of the Xbox configurations. Coming in a stylish and somehow sleeker-looking black matte finish, the Elite has a few bells and whistles that make it a smart buy for those who know they're going to use their Xbox 360 for media-related tasks or are avid about downloading demos.

The Elite comes complete with the following:

- Xbox 360 console.

- Standard AV cable.

- Component AV cable (for high-definition televisions).

- Wireless controller (black).

- Power cord and transformer.

- Ethernet cable.

- HDMI digital AV cable.

- 120 GB hard drive.

- Xbox Live wired headset.

- Xbox Live Silver membership (one-month trial Gold membership).

note Depending on the model of Xbox that you purchase, you may also get some included games. Of course, the special edition Xbox 360 Halo and Simpsons packages include the game associated with it.

Setting Up Your Xbox

Although the original Xbox and the Xbox 360 are based on PC technology, you don't have to worry about the complexities of PC hardware and software. In fact, it seems that Microsoft has learned something from Sony, Apple, and Nintendo about making the Xbox plug and play, which is a fancy way of saying that you just plug the Xbox in and it works. With an Xbox 360, there's a little more to it, but basically you can just plug it in to the wall, connect a few cables, and—voilà—you are good to go!

Despite the ease of use, it's still worth going through a quick how-to for setting up the Xbox 360 once it comes out of the box. For the purposes of this demonstration, we are going to use an Xbox 360 console with a wired controller, a wireless controller, an Ethernet cable, a standard/component AV cable, and even an optical audio cable for 5.1 Dolby Digital sound reproduction! I need to note here that the one cable not included with the Xbox 360 (with any model) is the optical audio cable. You can purchase one from Radio Shack or Best Buy, usually for less $10, and they look like the cable shown in **Figure 2.1.**

Figure 2.1
An optical audio cable for connecting the 360 to a Dolby Digital 5.1-capable amplifier/ speaker system.

A quick look at the Xbox

Let's take a quick visual tour of the Xbox 360 so we can see what each connector/space is for as well as where we are suppose to connect the cables and connectors (**Figure 2.2** and **Figure 2.3**).

Figure 2.2
The front of the
Xbox 360.

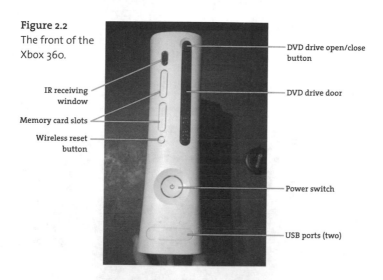

DVD drive open/close
button

DVD drive door

IR receiving
window

Memory card slots

Wireless reset
button

Power switch

USB ports (two)

Figure 2.3
The back of the
Xbox 360.

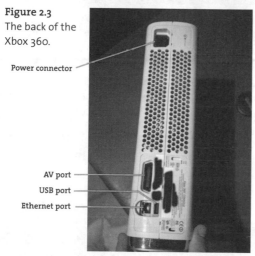

Power connector

AV port

USB port

Ethernet port

Making the connections

1. Start by unwrapping all of the pieces and setting them where you can put your hands on them immediately (**Figure 2.4**).

Figure 2.4
Lay out all of the parts somewhere so that you have easy access to every piece.

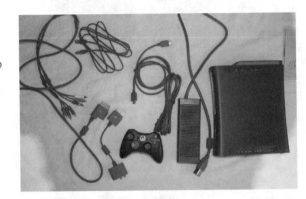

2. Connect the power cord.

First put the plug into the wall socket, then connect it to the transformer, and then plug the transformer to the 360 (**Figure 2.5**): This connection is a little bit different since there is a locking mechanism on it to ensure the power cable can't accidentally come free.

Figure 2.5
The connection to the 360 is tight and has a locking mechanism.

3. Next connect the AV cable to the back of the 360 (**FIGURE 2.6**).

Figure 2.6
Connect the AV cable to the back of the 360.

4. Now connect the AV cable to your television or monitor.

If you are connecting to a non-high-definition television, use the yellow video cable. If you going high-definition, then use the component connections (red, green, and blue; **FIGURE 2.7**).

Figure 2.7
Well, you can't really tell here, but these are the blue, green, and red connectors for high-definition video.

5. Next up, connect the optical digital audio cable to the small hole on the back of the AV cable (**FIGURE 2.8**). The other end goes into your Dolby Digital-capable amplifier or speaker system.

Figure 2.8
The digital audio optical connection is on the back of the AV cable.

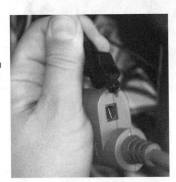

6. Connect the wired Xbox 360 controller to the USB port on the front of the 360 (**Figure 2.9**).

Figure 2.9
Open the small door at the front to find the two USB ports.

7. Connect the Ethernet cable to the back of the 360 and then to your cable modem or router (**Figure 2.10**).

Figure 2.10
You'll find a standard Ethernet cable connector on the back of all 360s.

8. The only thing left to do now is hit the power button on your 360, turn on the TV, and watch it fire up!

Video/display connections

The 360 is capable of outputting a video signal in standard NTSC format (television as we have known it for the last 50 years), but it can also output in high definition at 480p, 720p, 1080i, and 1080p, depending on the capability of your television/display. To display in high definition, the Xbox 360 requires that a special AV cable be connected to it. This cable has what's known as component video outputs, which is a fancy way of saying high-definition outputs. These cables are divided into red, green, and blue cables for the video signal (**Figure 2.11**) and a standard RCA red-and-white cable for the audio portion.

Figure 2.11 The component cable's three plugs divide the video signal into red, green, and blue components, allowing for high-definition signals to pass. This cable also has a standard video connector and right and left audio channels for non-HD situations.

To enjoy the high-definition (HD) capability of the 360, you need a television or monitor that can display HD. Some modern displays have a special digital interface known as an HDMI, or High-Definition Multimedia Interface, that allows for higher quality high-definition signals to pass between the 360 and the television/monitor. Only the Xbox 360 Elite comes with an HDMI cable (**Figure 2.12**) for the HDMI connector.

Figure 2.12
The HDMI connector that comes with an Xbox 360 Elite system.

You set up the video output from your 360 to your monitor/television on the Xbox 360 Dashboard. Here's how to set up the 360 to output in the format you require/desire:

1. In Dashboard, use the control stick on the controller to move to the System tab (**Figure 2.13**).

Figure 2.13
Get to the System tab in the Xbox Dashboard.

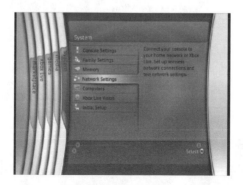

2. Select Console Settings and then select Display (**Figure 2.14**) from the menu (they're the two top selections in each screen).

Figure 2.14
Select Display.

3. Select HDTV Settings from the next menu (**Figure 2.15**).

Figure 2.15
Choose the HDTV Settings selection.

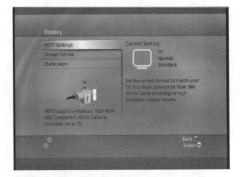

4. Now select from 480p, 720p, 1080i, or 1080p high definition output from your Xbox 360 to match the capability of your television/monitor (**Figure 2.16**).

Figure 2.16
Pick the output mode you want.

5. If you don't have an HD-capable television, then simply select TV Normal Standard in the Screen Format selection (**Figure 2.17**).

Figure 2.17
If you have a standard TV, then set it up in the Screen Format area.

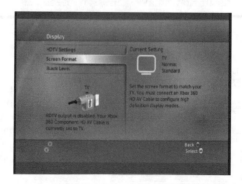

High-Definition Lingo

Since entire books have been written on the subject of high definition and the history and technology of television broadcasting, I'm going to boil this down into a sort of gooey mess that I'm hoping is understandable without using too much brain power.

Back in 1953 the NTSC (National Telecommunications Systems Committee) came up with the NTSC television broadcast standard that is still used today to bring television signals to our homes. As you might imagine, a technology and protocol designed more than half a century ago is probably not keeping up with changes in technology. In fact, when the NTSC broadcast standard became the norm, the concept of a man-made satellite orbiting the earth was pure fantasy, and now most of the television signals we watch are bounced off of such satellites!

But I digress ... This NTSC standard called for 525 vertical lines of information that would be displayed at 59.94 fields per second. A field is a set of lines of information on the screen and is either an even or odd. To break this down to its simplest form, the lines of information on the standard television screen (from a standard NTSC signal) are drawn line by line from the top down, but only every *second* line is drawn. After the first screen of lines is drawn (which consists of half the screen on every other line), the other set of lines are then drawn, thus filling in the blank spaces. So on one pass there are 263 lines drawn and on the second pass there are 262 lines drawn to give a total of 525 lines.

I know it seems complicated, but what I just said in the previous paragraph is that every 1/30th of a second the entire screen of information on your television is painted on. This every other line-by-line painting method used by the NTSC standard is what creates the flicker on a television screen. You can see this flicker if you stand far away from a TV and you are chewing gum or you video tape a television that's broadcasting. That line you see moving across the TV screen on the videotape of a TV is caused by this painting method.

OK, so fast-forward half a century and some pretty smart folks figured out that we could actually paint the lines on the screen all at the same time rather than every other line, thereby increasing the crispness and richness of the picture. This technology is called progressive scan and it was first introduced on DVD players (of course it's now a standard feature). The next leap from progressive scan is high definition, which increases the amount of information on the television's screen greatly and makes the picture much more vivid and clear. The forms of high definition are 480p (progressive scan at 480 lines), 720p (progressive scan at 720 lines), 1080i (1080 lines but drawn every other line like in NTSC) and 1080p (the highest-end picture, which paints all 1080 lines at once on the screen).

Compared to a standard NTSC signal, a 1080i high definition television displays nearly 700 percent (or seven times) the information of what the old TV signal displayed. No wonder it's crisper to look at! The Xbox 360 can display in every HD mode available, so if you have the TV or monitor to handle it, then go ahead and enjoy the fantastic visual fidelity of high-definition gaming.

Internet connection

Connecting to the Internet is usually a cinch. Basically, you connect one end of an Ethernet cable to the back of the Xbox 360 and then the other end to a cable/DSL modem, a cable/DSL gateway, or a router that's connected to your modem or gateway. In most cases, once you've made this simple link, the Xbox 360 figures out the rest by itself. In fact, 99.9 percent of the Xbox connections should work like a charm, and the Xbox handles everything automatically without your even lifting a finger.

However, since some folks are going to have problems, here is where you can find the network settings in case you need to add or change anything:

1. Go to the System tab and select Network Settings (**Figure 2.18**).

Figure 2.18
Select Network Settings from the System tab.

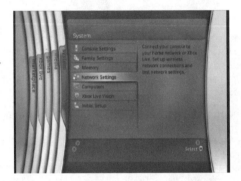

2. Then, go into the Edit Settings area and enter any key but missing networking information, such as IP address and gateway info (**Figure 2.19**). (If you don't know how to do this, don't sweat it: Your ISP will be happy to help).

Figure 2.19
If you need to get into the guts of your Internet connection you can here.

Wireless Internet connection

If you happen to have a computer that's already connected to the Internet and you've attached a wireless network adapter to your 360, then you can use a cool Xbox feature called Windows Connect Now (go ahead and select it from the Network Setting menu, as shown in **Figure 2.20**). This feature goes out and finds all of the information already on your PC and transfers it to the Xbox 360 console so that you don't have to! This will get your wireless networking up and running in a jiffy!

Figure 2.20
Windows Connect Now lets the 360 borrow wireless info from your PC to make the 360 connect to the wireless network.

Connecting a wireless controller

One of the great features of the Xbox 360 is its wireless controller (**Figure 2.21**). Hey, who hasn't ripped the entire console system out of its spot by accident on the way to get pizza or to visit the little gamer's room? With a wireless Xbox 360 controller, you can control everything from watching DVDs to playing games with the ease and convenience of wireless connections.

Figure 2.21
The front
and top of
the wireless
controller.

Start button   Right thumbstick

Xbox button   Y button   A button

Back button   X button   B button

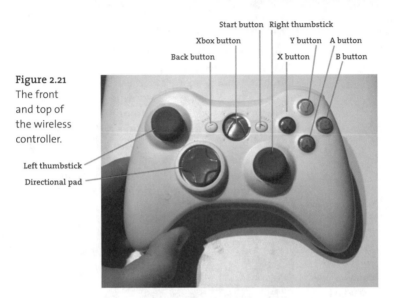

Left thumbstick
Directional pad

Left trigger   Wireless power pack   Right trigger

Left button   Expansion port   Right button

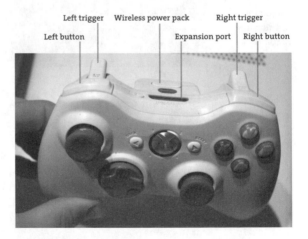

To connect a wireless controller to your 360, you need to make sure the controller is loaded up with batteries and turned on, and then all you do is press the Xbox Guide button (the button in the center of the controller with an X on it) as shown in **FIGURE 2.22.** When you do this (you need to hold the button down for a second or two) the ring of light around this button rotates and then stops once it's connected to the Xbox 360 wirelessly. It's pretty darned cool, and it works quickly and easily without any trouble. Once your controller is linked to your Xbox, you can control your 360 with it.

Figure 2.22
The wireless controller Xbox Guide button lights up when attached via a wireless connection.

note

If your wireless controller sits unattended for more than 15 minutes, it turns itself off to save power and displays a message on the screen telling you your controller has lost connection with the Xbox 360. Not to worry: Press the Xbox Guide button on the wireless controller, and you reconnect to the 360 immediately.

Headset connection

I discuss Xbox Live details Chapter 4, "Xbox Live," but if you want to connect the wired Xbox Live headset to your controller, you need only plug the headset into the expansion port of your wired or wireless controller (**Figure 2.23**).

Figure 2.23 Plugging the headset in to the controller is dead easy.

3

Gaming with the Xbox

I could be wrong, but I'm fairly sure that most folks don't go out to buy an Xbox 360 thinking "Wow, this is going to be *great* when I put my photos on it and download movie trailers!" In fact, I'm fairly sure that the Xbox 360 consoles people purchase are primarily for playing kick-ass games such as Halo 3 (**FIGURE 3.1**), and all of that other stuff is just nice fluffy extra goodness piled on top of the gaming sundae that is the Xbox 360.

Figure 3.1
Halo 3 is a
major reason
for owning an
Xbox 360.

note If, however, you are someone who bought your Xbox for its home media-center capabilities, check out Chapter 8, "The 360 as a Media Center."

Because games are so darned important to 360 users, this chapter looks exclusively at the top games for the 360 as well as several popular but unique games that have helped to change the gaming landscape. Since there are hundreds of Xbox 360 games and another couple of hundred older Xbox games, I'm not going to create an exhaustive list of the best games, complete with reviews of each. Since I'm assuming some of the folks reading this book are new to the Xbox, I'll to cover five of the best games for the 360 and then look at a couple of very popular games that are truly outside of the box.

note If you are interested in older Xbox games and their compatibility with the Xbox 360 then check out Chapter 5: "Backward Compatibility."

The Top Five Games

Of course, it's a matter of opinion which games are the best for any particular gaming platform, so if you don't agree with my choices, I hereby apologize. I arrived at this list of games by taking the top-five highest-rated games according to the most popular gaming magazines and Web sites. I focused on Xbox 360 games specifically, not Xbox games that can be played on the 360. I should also note that I've written about 75 strategy guides for computer and console games, so I know a bit about games.

So, after looking at the games in my personal library, the games my sons and their friends want to play, and the games that claim the highest rating on the most popular gaming Web sites, I came up with my list of top five games.

Halo and the Mac

A lot of people don't know this, but if it wasn't for the Macintosh, we might not have the Halo franchise. Bungie Software, maker of Halo, started out as a Macintosh gaming developer, producing such classic Mac games as Pathways Into Darkness and Marathon. If not for its considerable success on the Macintosh, Bungie Software might never have created Halo. So all those Halo fans out there can say thanks to the Mac for the rise of their favorite game.

Halo 3

Price: $59.99
Publisher: Microsoft
Genre: First-person shooter
Age rating: M for Mature
Number of players: 1 to 4

Halo 3 (**FIGURE 3.2**) is (as
the version number would
suggest) the third installment
in the Halo video game series.
Set in the Kenyan Savanna on futuristic earth, Halo
3 is a first-person shooting game that features spectacular graphics and stunning sound effects. Perhaps
the most impressive aspect of Halo is the multiplayer
gaming features that allow gamers to go online over
Xbox Live and play Halo 3 against other gamers the
world over.

Figure 3.2
Halo 3 is the
third and
arguably best of
an already great
series.

When playing multiplayer Halo 3 on one machine, as many as four players can join the battle using split-screen technology. Split screen basically means that the screen divides into four equal areas, each of which represent one player's space. If you have a local network set up with an Xbox 360 or you are connected via Xbox Live then up to 16 (count 'em) players can be involved simultaneously. Obviously, with rating points, a ranking system, and updated maps and bonus features, Halo 3 is a game that can be (and will be) played for many years to come by its fans. So if cartoon-level violence without blood is not a concern for you, then Halo 3 is definitely on the top of the list for an Xbox 360 owner.

Halo accessories

Halo 3 is such a big deal that a host of accessories are associated with the game. From Missile Cases to custom Halo 3 backpacks for kids to Halo headsets (**FIGURE 3.3**), Halo 3 has a slew of accessories for kids of all ages.

Figure 3.3
The Halo headset includes the Halo icon on the mic.

Perhaps the most practical of accessories are the Halo 3 wireless controllers that not only have a cool design on them but also come with a small Halo McFarlane action figure (**Figure 3.4** and **Figure 3.5**).

Figure 3.4
Thrilling Halo action right on your controller.

Figure 3.5
The Halo 3 controllers come with a posable Halo 3 figurine.

Halo History

Back in the mid 1990s I was working on a strategy guide for a game called Myth from Bungie Software in Chicago. At that time, Bungie was owned by Alexander Seropian and Jason Jones, the founders of Bungie. Near the end of my project, the producer for Myth (a Mac and PC real-time strategy game), Tuncer Deniz, invited me into the inner sanctum, where Jason Jones was showing off an extremely early version of what would ultimately become Halo.

At that time, Halo was, of course, different than what it ultimately would turn out to be, but the basic premise and look has remained the same.

The Halo franchise as we know it was born in the late 1990s when Microsoft purchased Bungie Software in a bid to make the highly anticipated Bungie game, Halo, an exclusive title for the new Xbox gaming console. With the release of the Xbox, Halo became a must-have game that, indeed, was so good that many gamers went out and bought an Xbox system just so that they could play the game. Halo's popularity was so great that when Halo 2 hit the streets in late 2004, it broke sales records for a video game release.

In October of 2007 Halo 3 sold over $150 million worth of units in the first 24 hours of release! All told, more than 20 million units of Halo games (most of them Xbox games) have been sold worldwide, making the Halo franchise one of the most successful ever.

BioShock

Price: $59.99
Publisher: 2K Games
Genre: Action RPG
Age rating: M for Mature
Number of players: 1 to 4

BioShock is a unique first-person-shooter/action RPG (role-playing game) experience that has been dubbed a Halo-killer by some, although it is different enough that the two shouldn't be compared. What's unique about BioShock (**Figure 3.6**) is that the gaming experience is unpredictable and occurs in real time. Perhaps the most refreshing aspect is that success doesn't just come from destroying a certain number of enemies; indeed, you must hack devices and make your own special items to find a path to success. Spectacular graphics and animations add to a story that involves making decisions such as whether to modify your own body to improve your chances of success. Lots of fun for the teenager or mature gamer.

Figure 3.6
BioShock is a fantastic game.

Madden NFL 08

Price: $59.99
Publisher: Electronic Arts
Genre: Sports
Age rating: E for Everyone
Number of players: 1 to 2

Nearly 20 years ago now the Madden football game burst onto the scene and quickly crushed all competition around it, no matter what platform the competitor was on. Fast forward to 2008, and Madden NFL 08 (**FIGURE 3.7**) continues to dominate the competition with fantastic gameplay and a slew of compelling features. Let's face it though, when it comes to football games, the actual gameplay and feel of the game is *everything*. Madden is fun to play, easy enough to learn for the novice, and has enough finesse controls for the aficionado to keep everyone happy.

Figure 3.7
Madden is still great after all these years.

The feature list for the latest incarnation of Madden is as follows:

- New Read & React system uses new player skill icons to help you identify on-field strengths and weaknesses so that you can create mismatches and exploit the opposing players.

- Front Office mode lets you build your own stadium, set everything from concession prices to seat size, hire a coaching staff, draft your players, and manage everything from the ground up.

- In-game championship ring design possible when Madden Gamer Level reaches a certain point.

- New acrobatic plays and animations.

- New ball-stripping tactics and defensive maneuvers make it possible to knock the ball loose with special bone-jarring hits in the secondary.

Elder Scrolls IV: Oblivion

Price: $29.99
Publisher: 2K Games
Genre: Role playing
Age rating: M for Mature
Number of players: 1

The Elder Scrolls is a long-standing role-playing gaming series. This latest incarnation has you taking control of a character's life in another world, choosing from myriad character attributes, ranging from a wizard-type character to a ninja-like assassin. Oblivion includes an exciting new magic and combat system that brings a new level of realism to the gameplay. Elder Scrolls IV is highly immersive, with bustling towns, dark dungeons, rich characters, and fantastic visuals and sound. The features for Oblivion include:

- Combat and magic system that combines RPG and first-person gaming elements.

- Complex artificial intelligence algorithms that allow in-game characters to make their own decisions.

- A huge gaming world exists for open-ended gameplay and hundreds of hours of exploration.

- More than one thousand supporting characters with lifelike animations and detailed speech populate the world of Elder Scrolls IV: Oblivion.

Forza Motorsport 2

Price: $59.99
Publisher: Microsoft
Genre: Car racing simulation
Age rating: E for Everyone
Number of players: 1

For those players who love car racing—or even for those folks who just love to drive cars— the latest class of racing games are so lifelike that it's hard to separate what you see in the game from real life! Forza Motorsport 2 is perhaps the finest racing game today on the Xbox 360, and it certainly begs for the purchase of one of the add-on racing wheels available for the 360. With more than 300 customizable cars and racetracks from the world over, Forza is a spectacular simulation with impossible camera angles that takes the player into the leading edge of real-life racing physics. The feature list of Forza 2 includes:

- Sixty-frame-per-second animation at 720p high definition for ultra-crisp realistic gameplay.

- Customize your car from the brakes and suspension to the engine.

- Cars are damaged and incur wear and tear during racing, and this factors into the game's physics, affecting races in real time.

- Xbox Live racing available so that you can race with people around the world.

- Alter the look of your car from decals to the paint job.

- More than 300 cars to collect/unlock and race. You can customize these cars after they become available.

Gaming Outside the Box

First, I'd like to apologize for even having to use the tired cliché "out of the box" in this book, but I just couldn't think of a better way to describe a couple of the games that are making waves in the gaming community. In fact, these games are not only having an impact in the gaming community but are altering the demographic landscape of gaming by drawing in folks who previously wouldn't have even looked at a video-game system for entertainment.

The two products I'm thinking of in particular use the Xbox 360 to expand the scope and breadth of what a gaming system can do. In the case of Dance Dance Revolution, it's helping people lose weight—of all things!—and in the case of Guitar Hero 2, it's letting people combine karaoke and air guitar into a blend of entertainment that's surprisingly fun.

Guitar Hero 2

Price: $59.99 (without guitar controller) $79.99 (with guitar controller)
Publisher: Activision
Genre: Guitar simulation
Age rating: T for Teen
Number of players: 1 to 2

Guitar Hero is a highly innovative game that takes real rock and roll music and combines it with a cool guitar controller (**Figure 3.8**). Basically, the screen becomes a giant fret board, with notes scrolling toward the player as the song plays (**Figure 3.9**). As the gamer hits or doesn't hit notes, the score changes accordingly. Surprisingly, as a reasonably qualified real-life guitar player, I have to admit that I enjoyed Guitar Hero 2 a heck of a lot more than I thought I would. Indeed, I even found that many of my real-life guitar skills come in handy, sparking my kids to say "whoa, dad, how do you do that?!?" In the end, it's remarkably addictive, and it's turned into a huge hit that has spawned many add-ons, wireless guitar controllers, gig bags, and plenty of other Guitar Hero accoutrements.

Figure 3.8
The notes come at you dynamically on a giant fret board.

Figure 3.9
The author attempting (and failing) to look cool with the guitar controller.

While Guitar Hero 2 is rated T for Teen, I can say with all honesty that I let my six- and eight-year-old sons play this game without any reservations. If you're looking for something that dad and mom can play with the school-age kids and have a blast, this game is high on the list—and I speak from experience!

Dance Dance Revolution Universe

Price: $39.99
Publisher: Konami
Genre: Dancing game/
exercise tool
Age rating: E for Everyone
(recommended 10+ years
of age)
Number of players: 1 to 4

Dance Dance Revolution (DDR) comes with its very
own controller: An especially adapted floor mat
with sensors in it that detect when the player steps
on specific areas of the mat. Originally designed as
merely an arcade game and released into arcades
worldwide in 1998 by Konami, DDR, as it's called
(**Figure 3.10**), became a surprise hit and got released
on the Dreamcast, Game Boy Color, PlayStation,
PlayStation 2, Xbox, GameCube, Xbox 360, and Wii
consoles.

Figure 3.10
On-screen with
DDR Universe.

Probably the most surprising offshoot of the DDR phenomenon is the fitness craze that's grown up around this game. For example, a number of over-weight high school students the world over did nothing else in their lives than play a couple of hours of DDR every day. The result was that these kids lost a lot of weight. Not surprisingly, news services such as MSNBC and CNN picked up on the craze and reported on it. Now there are fitness clubs with DDR machines as well as government-sponsored programs to help kids get fit using DDR (**Figure 3.11**), and let me and let me tell you, it makes you sweat!

Figure 3.11 The author's son doing his thing on the DDR Universe dance pad.

Other Great Games

This small section gives brief information about other highly rated Xbox 360 games that are worth looking into. While the cost of many games can be fairly prohibitive, I recommend checking out Blockbuster stores, where you can rent Xbox 360 games for an entire week for a fraction of the cost of buying the games. If you are unsure if you are going to like a game (or if your kids are going to like a game), $9 spent on a one-week rental is far easier on your pocketbook than $70 spent on a game that they/you may never play!

The Orange Box

Price: $59.99
Publisher: Electronic Arts
Genre: Action/adventure first-person shooter
Age rating: T for Teen + M for Mature
Number of players: 1

This combination of five classic games is based on the Half-Life saga (a very successful string of video games). Lots of classic fun that's guaranteed to entertain.

Gears of War

Price: $59.99
Publisher: Microsoft
Genre: Action/adventure first-person shooter
Age rating: M for Mature 17+
Number of players: 1 to 2

Gears of War is another classic game from the maker of the classic first-person shooters Unreal and Unreal Tournament. Gears of War is action-packed fun that's highly enjoyable if a bit violent.

Tom Clancy's Ghost Recon Advanced Warfighter

Price: $29.99
Publisher: Ubi Soft
Genre: First-person shooter
Age rating: T for Teen
Number of players: 1 to 4

The latest in the Ghost Recon first-person shooter series. The cool thing about the Ghost Recon games are the smooth communication channels for multiplayer action when playing with the Xbox Live system.

Puzzle Quest: Challenge of the Warlords

Price: $19.99
Publisher: D3 Publisher
Genre: Puzzle (Xbox Live Arcade)
Age rating: E for Everyone
Number of players: 1 to 2

A highly rated but simple puzzle game. Since the Xbox 360 is so dominated by first-person shooters—which let's face it, tend to be violent—why not dive into this game, which is rated 9 out of 10 or higher on at least half a dozen gaming sites.

Ace Combat 6: Fires of Liberation

Price: $59.99
Publisher: Namco
Genre: Flying
Age rating: T for Teen
Number of players: 1

A highly rated and exciting combat flight simulator for the 360, Ace Combat 6 also comes as a bundle with a special flight-stick joystick that's designed to function with this game. It's a lot of fun, and in cases like this, if there's a specialized controller, it's usually worth it.

Flatout: Ultimate Carnage

Price: $49.99
Publisher: Warner Bros.
Genre: Action/adventure first-person shooter
Age rating: M for Mature 17+
Number of players: 1

A scary-realistic racing/smashing car game that's so good you won't know if you're watching high-definition television of a race or the game itself! There's no split-screen mode here, but Xbox Live is a hoot. A racing wheel is a bonus for this one.

NHL 08

Price: $59.99
Publisher: Electronic Arts
Genre: Hockey/Sports
Age rating: E for Everyone 10+
Number of players: 1 to 4

For those ice-hockey fans, this is the one and only game for you. If you're Canadian, it's pretty much a must-have, but not to worry, because it's a blast to play and an excellent game that remains enjoyable even after a hundred matches.

NBA Street Homecourt

Price: $29.99
Publisher: Electronic Arts
Genre: Basketball/sports
Age rating: E for Everyone
Number of players: 1

Another great sporting
title from EA, NBA Street
Homecourt allows you to start
at the bottom in the neighborhood and work all the
way up to the NBA. Not really a great multiplayer
experience but a ton of fun for basketball fans.

Battlestations: Midway

Price: $39.99
Publisher: Eidos
Genre: War simulation
Age rating: T for Teen
Number of players: 1

This is a fantastic simulation
of the Battle of Midway in the
Pacific. You can get involved
on a ship, in an aircraft, or just sit back and manage
the entire thing. It's a lot of fun but has a fairly long
learning curve.

NBA Live 08

Price: $59.99
Publisher: Electronic Arts
Genre: Basketball/sports
Age rating: E for Everyone
Number of players: 1 to 2

If you like the multiplayer high-end basketball action, then EA has got all you want right here with this game!

Tony Hawk's Proving Ground

Price: $59.99
Publisher: Activision
Genre: Skateboarding/sports
Age rating: T for Teen
Number of players: 1to 2

Lots of kids and teens idolize Tony Hawk, and why not: The guy's amazing! Tony Hawk has had some highly rated and very fun video games over the last few years, and this one is no different, taking full advantage of the 360's raw power.

A noncomprehensive list

Games are coming out every week, and it's nearly impossible to keep up, but this list gives you an idea of some of the good games out there and what kind of a game they are. In terms of ratings, I haven't included any game with a rating that's lower than 7 out of 10 or 3.5 stars out of 5, as rated by leading game magazines and sites.

Sports

- 2006 FIFA World Cup
- 3D Ultra Minigolf Adventures
- Bankshot Billiards 2
- FIFA Soccer 08
- Fight Night Round 3
- Major League Baseball 2K7
- NCAA Football 08
- NHL 2K8
- Pro Evolution Soccer 2008
- Skate
- Tiger Woods PGA Tour 08
- Tony Hawk's American Wasteland
- Tony Hawk's Project 8
- Top Spin 2

Action/arcade

- Assault Heroes
- Bionicle Heroes
- Crackdown
- Lego Star Wars II: The Original Trilogy
- Lost Planet: Extreme Condition
- Prince of Persia Classic
- Sonic the Hedgehog 2
- Streets of Rage 2

Shooters

- Call of Duty 2
- Call of Duty 3
- Every Extend Extra Extreme
- F.E.A.R.
- Far Cry Instincts Predator
- Halo 2
- Medal of Honor: Airborne
- Perfect Dark Zero
- Prey
- Tom Clancy's Rainbow Six: Vegas

Role-playing games (RPG)

- Blue Dragon
- Elder Scrolls IV: The Shivering Isles
- Enchanted Arms
- Eternal Sonata
- Final Fantasy XI
- Phantasy Star Universe
- The Godfather
- Two Worlds

Racing games

- DiRT
- Juiced 2: Hot Import Nights
- Mad Tracks
- MotoGP '07
- NASCAR 08
- Project Gotham Racing 3
- Ridge Racer 6

Simulations

- Armored Core 4
- Outpost Kaloki X
- Thrillville: Off the Rails
- Viva Pinata

Strategy games

- Carcassonne
- Catan
- Command & Conquer 3 Tiberium Wars
- Lord of the Rings: The Battle for Middle-Earth II
- Worms

4

Xbox Live

In the highly competitive and cutthroat world of video game consoles, what ultimately has kept consoles such as the Xbox alive and popular is the ability for gamers to get online and play games with others the world over. Xbox Live not only allows gamers to connect and play against one another in a variety of gaming environments but also gives the user access to chat rooms, ratings systems, instant messaging, video chat, and a plethora of online content from movie trailers to game demos.

This chapter takes a look at the Xbox Live environment and its various capabilities as they apply to the average Xbox 360 user as well as the online aficionado. Whether you just want to go online and play a little Call of Duty 3 against a few friends once in a while or you want to hook up the Xbox video camera and do some video chatting with someone in Walla Walla, Washington, this chapter shows you the basics of how to get started.

High-Speed Internet

Probably the single most important change in technology that's allowed services such as Xbox Live to flourish is the move to high-speed Internet connections in households. No matter how efficient dial-up connections become, the technology is inherently just too slow and cumbersome to move the large amounts of data necessary to make online multiplayer gaming workable and enjoyable.

The gradual shift to reliable and relatively inexpensive high-speed Internet connections has meant that gamers nearly anywhere can enjoy playing online games at any time without having to go through a lot of painful dial tones and connection issues. If you don't have a high-speed connection and you want to get on board with Xbox Live, then you are going to want to join the party (so to speak) and get yourself a high-speed connection of some sort.

What Exactly Is Xbox Live?

Xbox Live is an online gaming environment that also delivers specialized content via the Internet. It is operated and owned by Microsoft and exists to support the Xbox and the Xbox 360 gaming consoles. Xbox Live first came into being in late 2002 for the Xbox console and has continued to grow in both size and scope ever since. Today Xbox Live is geared toward the Xbox 360 console system, and it adds to the gaming experience on the Xbox 360 and to the functionality of the console.

Here's the basic feature list of Xbox Live:

- Offers voice chat during online gameplay via the Xbox Live headset.

- Provides instant messaging.

- Handles video chat via the Xbox Live Vision Camera.

- Connects the user to their friends who are also on Xbox Live, displaying what game you are playing and what you are doing online at any given time.

- Includes avatars or gamer photos so that people can associate themselves with either an image or a real photo of themselves.

- Tracks gamer reputation and player achievements over the entire lifetime of a Xbox Live account.

- Allows access to the Xbox Live Marketplace and its content.

- Shows the last 50 players you engaged with and allows you to contact them if desired.

- Includes specific Gamer Zones that help to match up players with those who have similar likes and desires. There are four zones: Recreation, Pro, Family, and Underground.

- Allows online play with gamers from around the world.

Xbox Live pricing

Xbox Live offers Silver and Gold levels. Silver memberships are free and anyone can have one, and players can use a membership to play online against others and enjoy some but not all Xbox Live features. Gold is the paid membership and of course offers more to the user.

A monthly Gold subscription is $7.99 per month in the U.S. and $8.99 per month in Canada (although with the U.S. dollar's value being below that of Canada's, the pricing is odd). Users can subscribe per month, or they can sign up in 3-month chunks or even for 1 year. There is a significant saving for signing up long term.

Silver membership

Here's what you get with the free Silver membership:

- Create and maintain a friends list.

- Create a gamer profile.

- Send and receive text and voice messages.

- Access massively multiplayer games.

- Join in special Xbox Live Gold Trial opportunities.

- Access Xbox Live Marketplace, including Xbox Live Arcade, demos and trailers.

Gold membership

The Gold membership includes all that comes with the Silver membership and adds some more features:

- Online multiplayer gaming.

- Exclusive and early access to material on Xbox Live Marketplace.

- TrueSkill matchmaking.

- Enhanced gamer feedback.

- Enhanced friends-list management.

- Video chat.

Xbox Live Marketplace

The Xbox Live Marketplace is your virtual Xbox shopping mall that uses an online currency called Microsoft Points. Ultimately these points boil down to dollars and cents: You purchase points online with a credit card or by redeeming a prepaid gift card. The upside to the points system is that you don't have to enter credit-card numbers for each purchase you make but can, instead, can just buy items or features using the Microsoft Points system. Check out Chapter 6, "Shopping on Xbox Live," for details on how to buy points and items in the marketplace.

Live Gaming with Xbox Live

Many games that you purchase for the Xbox 360 are ready to go with the Xbox Live system, so once you have an Xbox Live account, you're all set. When you play a game that can take advantage of Xbox Live online gaming, connecting to Xbox Live and playing with gamers is automatically presented as an option (**Figure 4.1**).

Figure 4.1
Getting ready to connect in Xbox Live in the game Two Worlds.

Once you are playing a game online with your fellow gamers, be they opponents or cooperative players, you can chat with them via a headset (**Figure 4.2**) or with an Xbox 360 Messenger Kit (**Figure 4.3**), which also lets you type messages.

Without a doubt, human cohorts or opponents are infinitely more satisfying than playing with or against computer-generated players, so getting together online with gamers makes the experience much more interesting and dynamic. You just can't predict 100 percent of the time what a real person is going to do at any given moment, so even though you may think you have a human opponent's strategy down, that's the time when they throw caution to the wind and do something completely unexpected. And that, my friends, is what makes multiplayer gaming on Xbox Live such a blast!

Figure 4.2
A headset
microphone.

Figure 4.3
The Xbox 360
Communicator
Kit.

Voice communication via a headset

You can choose from two types of headsets for the Xbox 360, the standard wired headset and the wireless headset. I discuss each of these units in Chapter 7, "Xbox 360 Accessories," so I won't go into detail here. Suffice to say, however, that when one is playing a game of Call of Duty 3 and the goal is to rally allied troops to capture a German bunker, being able to call out to your companions and tell them exactly what needs to be done makes the gaming experience much closer to a real-life experience and therefore infinitely more enthralling than playing without such communication. In short, it rocks!

Playing games with voice communication via a headset is something that every gamer should experience. While obviously some games lend themselves to the technology more than others, there can be huge advantages to being able to communicate verbally while gaming even if it means that all you are doing is taunting your enemies.

Connecting the headset

Connecting the Xbox 360 Headset (the wired headset) to your controller is a snap. All you need to do is plug the headset's connector in to the expansion port on the controller (**Figure 4.4**). That's it! Once you start playing an Xbox Live game, the voice communication starts immediately as long as the mute button (**Figure 4.5**) isn't turned on.

Figure 4.4
The wired headset connects via the expansion port on the controller.

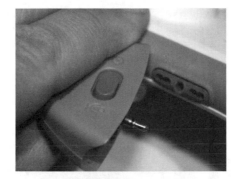

Figure 4.5
The mute button turns off the output of the headset.

Communication with Xbox Live

Xbox Live also connects you to the gaming/Xbox Live community. You can contact players whom you enjoy playing with, send them messages, and chat with them. It allows you to actually meet the people you're playing with.

tip When you play an online game on Xbox Live, the players you played against automatically are logged as potential friends in the Players area of the Community screen. This is an excellent way to get a chance to meet other folks with similar interests on Xbox Live.

Sending messages

One fun aspect of Xbox Live is that you can send messages to other gamers or friends. Sending messages is easy: If you already know a player's Gamertag, or online name, you can send them a message directly. But Xbox Live keeps track of who you have played games with, and so you can also chat with those players you share an interest with by sending them a message from the Players area of the Community menu (**Figure 4.6**).

Figure 4.6
You can send messages to other players or friends through the Community menu.

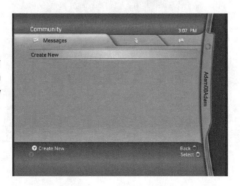

Meeting players

As you play a game on Xbox Live, it keeps track of
whom you play and interact with. Xbox tracks these
Gamertags as recent players in the Community
section of the Xbox Live area (**Figure 4.7**), and it's
here that you can reach out to gamers you enjoyed
playing with, requesting them to become your friends.

Figure 4.7
In the Community area
you can track down
people that you recently
played with and reach
out to them to see if
they'd like to play again—
or even chat with you.

Chatting or sending IMs

Another cool aspect of Xbox Live is its chat rooms,
video chat rooms, and even instant-messaging capabilities that allow you to contact your friends directly
and chat with them (**Figure 4.8**). Of course, you can
chat using the Xbox Communicator device, but you
can also connect via the Xbox Live Vision camera and
have face-to-face chats (**Figure 4.9**).

Figure 4.8
The Chat and
IM screen.

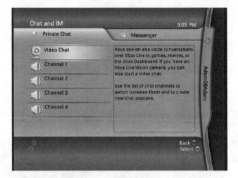

Figure 4.9
If you have
an Xbox Live
Vision camera,
you can chat
with your
friends face
to face (so to
speak).

Xbox Live Terms and Lingo

Xbox Live can be a foreign environment to many of
us when we first see it close up, so it can help to get
an idea of just what all of the words and concepts
mean. The section aims to help you to understand
what each of these terms is and what it means to
you, the Xbox Live gamer/user.

Xbox Live Marketplace

The virtual marketplace for Xbox Live allows you to spend Microsoft Points to purchase Xbox 360 games as well as other content. Check out Chapter 6, "Shopping on Xbox Live," for more information on Microsoft Points.

Windows Live Messenger on the Xbox 360

This is a connection point that allows Xbox Live users to meet and chat with Windows Live Messenger users. The best way to use this system is with the Xbox 360 Communicator Kit, which basically puts a QWERTY keyboard on your Xbox controller (see Chapter 7, "Xbox Accessories").

Gamertag

Your Gamertag is the name of your Xbox Live persona. Once this is set, that's it, it's you! With a Gamertag, others can contact you and send you messages any time that you are in Xbox Live. Your Gamertag also works with your Windows Live or Zune account, if you have one.

Gamerscore

Your Gamerscore is a measure of the number of gaming achievements that you have acquired during your time playing on the Xbox 360. Every game on the Xbox 360 has specific game challenges that are tied to these achievements and are kept track of by Xbox Live. Basically, the higher a person's Gamerscore, the better the gamer they appear to be. Gamerscore is a de facto status symbol.

Gamercard

The Gamercard is an information area in Xbox Live that shows the Gamertag, the Gamerscore, the Reputation of that player, and the Gamer Zone they inhabit. It's an all-in-one spot to get a read on what that player has done, where they hang, and what they're capable of.

TrueSkill

TrueSkill is relatively new to the Xbox 360 and is a skill-based ranking system that lets you find a good match when you play. The TrueSkill system uses several factors to determine a player's skill level, giving that person a huge status symbol if their TrueSkill level is high. It's a great way for gamers to see what they're up against when facing off against otherwise unknown players in Xbox Live.

Xbox Live Vision

This camera system is available as an accessory. It does, however, enable some camera-enabled games to be played, such as UNO and World Series of Poker. More on this in Chapter 7, "Xbox Accessories."

Xbox Live Arcade

The Xbox Live Arcade allows users to download arcade games directly to the hard drives of their Xbox 360 consoles. These games are usually smaller arcade-type games, with many of them having a distinctly retro-feel. Xbox Live Arcade (**Figure 4.10**) is a fun place to spend a few bucks and get some cool quick games to fool around with on your 360.

Figure 4.10
The Xbox Live Arcade area.

Setting up an Xbox Live Account

So you've decided to take the plunge and get an Xbox Live account, but you're not exactly sure how; fortunately, the process is dead-easy, but for the sake of making it even easier, I'll map out the process right here for you now.

1. Start by selecting the Xbox Live area from the Xbox Live tab (**Figure 4.11**).

Figure 4.11
Move to the Xbox Live tab (it lies between the Marketplace tab and the Games tab).

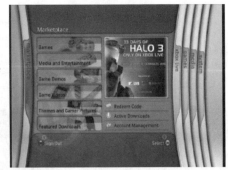

2. Next up, select Join Xbox Live. When you do this, you get to the Welcome to Xbox Live screen, where you select Continue (**Figure 4.12**).

Figure 4.12
Get started with the signup.

3. If you don't already have an Xbox Live ID, you'll have to create one. It's a necessary step (**Figure 4.13**).

Figure 4.13
If you don't have a Windows Live ID, you soon will.

4. You must select your country (**Figure 4.14**).

Figure 4.14
Choose the country in which you reside.

5. Then you must set your Windows Live ID, with an e-mail address and a password (**Figure 4.15**).

Be sure to answer a secret question.

Figure 4.15
Set up the Windows Live ID, including answering the secret question.

6. Now enter your date of birth, your name, credit card number, and address (**Figure 4.16**).

Figure 4.16
Set up the credit card information, address, and so on.

note If you are setting the account up as a child or for a child, you must have a parent's permission, and a parent's credit card number, and some of parental personal information to proceed.

7. Set a few more details, such as your parental settings (see **Figure 4.17**).

Figure 4.17
Choose the level of access your children will have to Xbox Live.

8. Finally you have to accept Microsoft's terms.

Once this is done, you're all set (see **Figure 4.18**)!

Figure 4.18
When you're finished you can move right into Xbox Live.

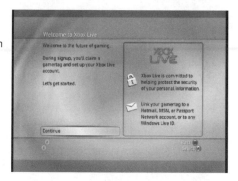

5

Backward Compatibility (Xbox Games)

One aspect of the current generation of video game systems is that you can (for the most part) play games created for the previous system on them. For example, the PlayStation 2 plays almost all of the games created for the original PlayStation, and most GameCube games work perfectly on the Nintendo Wii. This backward compatibility (as it is called) is highly attractive to console owners because, let's face it, we don't want to have to lose an investment that can amount to hundreds or thousands of dollars in video games for an older console.

For example, if someone owns an original Xbox and they bought 25 games for it over the years, that means that they likely spent in the neighborhood of $1,500 on those games. If buying an Xbox 360 meant that all of those old games would become unusable, then the desire to upgrade to the next-generation game console isn't nearly as strong. Fortunately for Xbox gamers, the Xbox 360 does offer a reasonable amount of backward compatibility, and that's what is examined in this chapter.

Backward Compatibility Defined

Backward Compatibility is, quite simply, the capability of a newer gaming system to run and use the games and peripherals that were created for that system's predecessor. In other words, a system that is fully backward compatible can play all of the games designed for its predecessor and also use all of the controllers and peripherals that were available to it (such as racing wheels and special joysticks.).

Xbox Game Compatibility

The Xbox 360 is indeed backward compatible with original Xbox games, but it isn't *100 percent* backward compatible with the entire Xbox catalogue of games. Because the Xbox 360 architecture differs so much from the original Xbox in terms of its processor and graphics card, the earlier Xbox games that do run on it have to run in emulation, which means that the Xbox 360 uses its considerable brain power to pretend that it's an original Xbox (**Figure 5.1**) to run the game in question.

Figure 5.1
An original Xbox
in all its glory.

Microsoft's compatibility plan is to start with the best-selling and most popular original Xbox games (**FIGURE 5.2**), but you will find less popular games on the compatibility list too. Microsoft said as it focuses on the top sellers, it finds less popular games that share similar architectures to the games it is working on, and so the Xbox 360 team includes those games on the compatibility list too (see Appendix A for the list).

Figure 5.2
Popular Xbox
games such
as Halo 2 were
among the first
to work on the
Xbox 360.

To enjoy backward compatibility with Xbox games, your Xbox 360 must have a hard drive in place. Without a hard drive, the Xbox 360 cannot access the necessary software it uses to ensure that backward-compatible Xbox games can play. The other wrinkle in this is that it's best if your Xbox 360 is connected to the Internet via a broadband connection because the system must download special updates to your 360's hard drive for many older Xbox games to run on your machine.

Updates

You may find that when you play an older Xbox game on your 360, it will work just fine—in fact, it may work exactly like it did on your old Xbox. Often, however, you will get a message from your Xbox 360 that says something like "This original Xbox game is not supported on your Xbox 360 console" (**Figure 5.3**). If you get this message, you can follow the on-screen directions to see if updates are available or not.

Figure 5.3
Uh oh, this older Xbox game doesn't want to work on the 360.

Automatic updates

You won't find updates for specific games; instead, you will see general updates that allow groups of older Xbox games to play on the 360. Hopefully, an update will then let you play the game you want on the 360. The Xbox 360 automatically looks for updates when you log in to Xbox Live in the Xbox Dashboard, but you have alternative ways to see if there is an update available. To check for an update online, go to http://www.xbox.com/en-CA/support/ in Canada or http://www.xbox.com/en-US/support/ in the United States.

Updating from a CD or DVD

If you have a home computer with an Internet connection, a CD or DVD burner, and a blank, writable CD or DVD, then you can create a CD or DVD to update your Xbox.

1. Go to Xbox.com, search for *Original Xbox Game Support*, and then locate and click the update link to download the update (**Figure 5.4**).

    The update is usually around 15 MB.

Figure 5.4
We've found our update and are ready to download it.

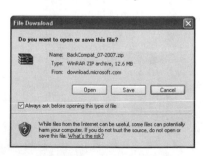

2. Unzip the file by double-clicking it (Windows XP or Vista) or manually unzipping it using WinZip (Windows ME or Windows 2000).

3. Once the file is unzipped, it's critical that the file is named default.xex. If it is not named this way, change its name (**Figure 5.5**).

Figure 5.5
That looks like the right file.

4. Place the blank DVD or CD in the burner.

5. Select Open writable CD folder using Windows Explorer or open the CD by double-clicking it in the window (**Figure 5.6**).

Figure 5.6
Make your selection.

6. Now drag the file named default.xex to the CD folder.

7. Click Write files to CD from the CD writing tasks in the Windows Explorer window or from the menu that appears when you right-click with your mouse.

8. Follow the CD/DVD wizard instructions to create the CD—it's all set up step by step (**Figure 5.7**).

Figure 5.7
Now, let's create a CD.

9. Once the CD/DVD is ready, place it in the Xbox 360 drive.

    The update program will start automatically.

10. Select Continue from the Apply Updater screen to install the update on the Xbox 360.

11. Once the update is complete, you will get a message that says an update must be applied to your console to play the game. in the Update Required window, select Yes, update now, and you're all set!

Ordering a CD Directly from Microsoft

If you don't have a computer to burn your own update CD or you don't feel like doing it, you can order an update CD from Microsoft (search for *Order the Original Xbox Games Support CD* on the www.xbox.com site) and have it delivered to your home for a small cost. When I went through the process of ordering an update CD, the cost was a whopping $0.00 (that's not a typo, the cost was actually zero). I'd say the price is right!

Practical problems

Be aware: The Xbox 360 may have problems working with and playing older Xbox games. Probably the biggest potential problem is that games may run a little slow or display chunky or broken-up images at times. These problems, thankfully, are uncommon, and for the most part, old games that are compatible with the Xbox 360 run just fine.

So which games work?

The next logical question is "Which old Xbox games work on the Xbox 360?" I'll start the answer by saying that Microsoft is constantly working on adding older titles to the compatible list, and its official stance is that eventually it will make every game backward compatible. We'll see if that actually comes to pass, but until then, Microsoft keeps an official list of games that run on the Xbox 360 here: http://www.xbox.com/en-US/games/backwardcompatibilitygameslist.htm. (You can find the list in Appendix A in this book.)

You can also find unofficial lists on the Internet by searching for *xbox compatible games list.*

 note | While the game you want to play might not be on the official list, it may just still work on the 360 anyway, so it's always worth giving it a try. One never knows if a game is going to work or not. Granted, if it's not on the list, it's likely that it won't work, but there are examples of some nonlist titles that seem to run just fine.

The "wait and see" approach

If you have an existing stockpile of original Xbox games (**FIGURE 5.8**) sitting in your garage, hold on to them because Microsoft is always adding older Xbox games to its Xbox updates, making those games playable on the Xbox 360. If you are going out and looking for secondhand Xbox games to snap up, then I'd recommend taking this book with you or printing the latest list of working games so that you can choose games that you know can run on your 360.

Figure 5.8
I have a bunch of old Xbox games, some of which won't run on the 360, but I keep them around anyway because eventually they may work.

Emulation

The Xbox 360 is able to play Xbox games through a process of *software emulation:* The 360 uses its prodigious processing power to *pretend* that it's an original Xbox and run Xbox games as if it were an original Xbox unit itself. Unfortunately, since the architecture used to create the original Xbox games varied widely, Microsoft needs to constantly update the software that emulates the original Xbox so that it can include additional games, and that takes time. As Microsoft tweaks the software with each update, more games become available to play on the 360.

6

Shopping with the Xbox 360

While shopping on the Xbox 360 isn't exactly as comprehensive as what you can do on systems such as the Nintendo Wii, you can still find a lot of the items on your shopping list in the Xbox Live Marketplace. This chapter takes a look at how to purchase Microsoft Points and buy content from the Xbox Live Marketplace while online with your Xbox 360.

The Xbox 360 As a Web Browser

While Microsoft doesn't really intend for you to use your Xbox to browse the Web, if you are really gung ho to use your 360 as a Web browser, there is a workaround that can have you surfing on your 360—provided that you have a few prerequisites.

You need a local network set up in your home (wireless or wired will do), a Windows PC with Windows Media Center 2005, and an Xbox 360 and all of the various accoutrements that are required to make said system run.

To get the scoop on how to do this, check out this post on an Xbox forum, http://forums.afterdawn.com/thread_view.cfm/426398, for a step-by-step tutorial on how to get your Xbox 360 surfing the Web—and presumably shopping. That said, if you have a Windows PC that's running Media Center 2005, then you have an Internet appliance that can access the Web anyway!

Marketplace Home

The Xbox Live Marketplace (**Figure 6.1**) is a one of the five main areas in the Xbox 360 interface. Let's take a little tour through the nine available selections in the Xbox Live Marketplace menu.

Figure 6.1
The Xbox Live Marketplace area in the 360's interface.

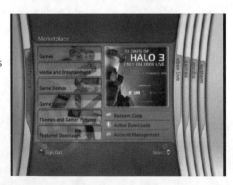

Games

The Games area offers five categories designed to help you find the games that interest you the most (**Figure 6.2**).

Figure 6.2
The Games area in the Marketplace.

> **note** Note the advertisements present in all of the Xbox Live areas. If you click to select one of these ads, you are taken to the game that the advertisement is pushing. It's a handy way to take a look at the information on a game that catches your eye, and if you want, you can then buy the game right from that window.

The five categories:

- **New Arrivals.** This area shows you the most recent games added to the Games area (**Figure 6.3**). Microsoft adds games routinely, so it's not uncommon to see a new title there every day or two.

Figure 6.3
The New
Arrivals area
is constantly
updated with
new games.

- **Xbox Live Arcade.** This area contains only Xbox
  Live Arcade games, which means the games only
  work online in Xbox Live. This is a special brand of
  games, often arcade style, designed to be played
  online with a group of Xbox Live gamers.

- **Played Games.** This is quite simply a running
  list of games you have played on Xbox Live in
  the past (**FIGURE 6.4**). It allows you to log in and
  play those same games again without searching
  for them.

Figure 6.4
A list of games
played on Xbox
Live in the past.

- **Genres.** This area breaks games down into one of fourteen categories, including Action, Adventure, Family, Fighting, Music, Platform, Racing, Role Playing, and even Xbox Live games. Pick the genre you want to play (**Figure 6.5**), and you will see the games in that genre listed.

Figure 6.5
You have 14 genres to choose from.

- **All Games.** This is, as you might suspect, a list of all games available on Xbox Live. My current list includes 306 games, so there's plenty to have a look at.

When you select a game from one of the lists in the Games area, you won't necessarily get to play that game. Indeed, if you select a game that you don't own, such as Pirates of the Caribbean: At World's End, you are given three options: You can see a demo of the game, view a making-of movie in high definition at 720p, or watch the game trailer in high definition (**Figure 6.6**). For Pirates of the Caribbean, all of these options are free, but if they weren't, you would see a cost associated with the option listed in Microsoft Points.

Figure 6.6
Often if you select a game, you get access to free demos, movies, and trailers relating to the game itself.

Media and Entertainment

The Media and Entertainment area contains five interesting categories that offer a wide range of content—from movies of actual gameplay to high-quality strategy guides for sale online. Here are the categories:

- **Movies and Short Films.** This catch-all area contains a wide variety of video, from advertisements to short films with an artsy quality. It's worth checking out, from time to time, to see what's there (**Figure 6.7**).

- **TV, Music Videos, and More.** Here you'll find television shows, music videos, and other content that would otherwise not fit anywhere else (**Figure 6.8**).

Figure 6.7
You never know what movies show up in here.

Figure 6.8
Right now a couple of television shows are available.

 The content available in some of these areas can vary depending on what type of gamer you said you were when you created your Xbox Live account.

- **Game Videos.** This area usually has plenty of gaming videos (**Figure 6.9**) to peruse and view for free. It's a great way to sample live gameplay without actually playing the game.

Figure 6.9
You can usually finds lots of gaming videos available.

- **Gaming Community Videos.** Here's where to find things such news reports on gaming, E3 reports (**Figure 6.10**), and other industry gossip in the form of newscast-like videos.

Figure 6.10
Community videos offer lots information about gaming.

- **Game Tips and Support.** Not surprisingly, this area has a selection of strategy guide chapters and tips (**Figure 6.11**) available to view. You can often buy content here one chapter at a time for 50 Microsoft Points each.

Figure 6.11
There are even online strategy guides available!

Game Demos

Straight up, this area is a clearinghouse of all of the game demos out there. If you want to check out a game demo, then this is the place to find it, look up its info, and decide if you want it to download it (**Figure 6.12**). Nearly all of the game demos here are free, but once in a while you get a demo that has a small cost associated with it. Usually the reason for the charge is that the demo is an especially large and playable area of a game.

Figure 6.12
Most of the demos are free for download.

If you choose to download a demo, you are taken to the standard purchase screen (**FIGURE 6.13**), but when you look at the price you usually see that it's free and you can simply start the download process.

Figure 6.13
Even free demos go through a purchase screen.

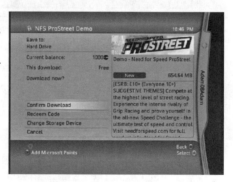

Game Videos

The Game Videos section includes a collection of commercially produced game videos for the hottest games and newest releases available. As a general rule, this content is duplicated in the Game Videos area of the Media and Entertainment page, but either way it's just another access point to this content.

Themes and Gamer Pictures

Purchase new and cool Xbox 360 themes here as well as avatars for your Gamertag (the little picture that appears beside your name). You can often find cool picture packs available. Buy most of the content here with Microsoft Points, and the costs are usually nominal (**Figure 6.14**).

Figure 6.14
You can usually find lots of new gamer pictures and theme sets available for purchase.

Featured Downloads

The Featured Downloads area contains whatever downloads the Xbox Live crew feels are worth highlighting. This is usually worth looking at since some of the downloads are of the hottest games. Some may cost you because they are not always demos; sometimes they are add-on capabilities for existing games (**Figure 6.15**).

Figure 6.15
The number of featured downloads available varies wildly as does the cost of the downloads themselves (from nothing to a thousand points).

Downloading Content

When you decide to download a music video, a game video, or even a game demo or two, you can download them simultaneously and then look at them in the Active Downloads area (**Figure 6.16**) of the Xbox Live Marketplace area. This area shows you how many active downloads are underway and what the status of each download is. It's a very handy feature!

Figure 6.16
The Active Downloads area shows you the progress on your current downloads.

Microsoft Points

Microsoft Points are the currency system of record in the Xbox Live Marketplace area. The original idea behind Microsoft Points was to eliminate a lot of credit card data entry and time-consuming transactions. You can purchase points online with a credit card. And anyone with cash can purchase prepaid Microsoft Points cards in a brick-and-mortar store (**Figure 6.17**). With one of the prepaid cards, users of any age can get points and use them to purchase games and other commodities online in the Xbox Live Marketplace.

Figure 6.17
A 1,400 Microsoft Points prepaid card I purchased to write this book.

Microsoft Points are worth 1.25 cents (U.S.) per point. Therefore, 100 points costs $1.25 and 5,000 points costs $62.50. Many games in the Xbox Live catalogue cost around 800 points, which works out to about $10 per game. Not bad for many of the games offered actually!

Adding Microsoft Points

You have several ways to add points to your account. First, you can buy a Microsoft Points card from a store and then simply enter the code into the appropriate fields in the Xbox Live Marketplace, or you can actually add points to your account by purchasing them online using a credit card.

1. Select the item that you want to purchase, and then hit the X button (it appears at the bottom of the screen and says Add Microsoft Points next to it; **Figure 6.18**).

Figure 6.18
The Add Microsoft Points option appears as an X button at the bottom of the screen.

2. You are taken to the Add Microsoft Points screen, where you can select from adding 500 points to adding 5,000 points (**Figure 6.19**).

Select the amount you want to buy.

Figure 6.19
Select the amount of points you want to purchase.

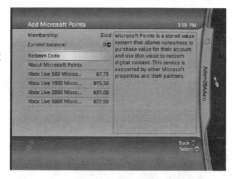

3. You can use the credit card on file or enter a new credit card.

Using the one on file is, obviously, easier, and faster (**Figure 6.20**).

Figure 6.20
Use the credit card on file if it's convenient.

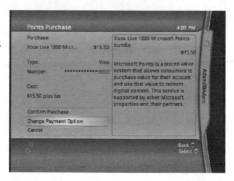

4. Once you confirm the purchase, you get a screen saying that the points have been added to your account (**Figure 6.21**). Voilà! You're now ready to spend again!

Figure 6.21 When you get the confirmation screen you know it's done.

7

Xbox Accessories

The Xbox 360 has been around just long enough—
and is certainly successful enough—that it has
collected a host of accessories that aim to improve
your experience with the console. While you can
turn your nose up at the idea of accessories for an
already-expensive device such as the Xbox 360,
you may find good reasons to purchase some of
these accessories. This chapter takes a look at the
Microsoft-branded accessories as well as a few of the
most popular third-party accessories available as I
write this book.

Microsoft Accessories

Let's first take a look at the accessories made available directly from mother Microsoft. These devices have the official Microsoft stamp of approval and are often associated with particular games such as Halo 3. The bottom line is that Microsoft-branded accessories are often useful items, whereas some of the third-party items are perhaps a little more vanity oriented.

Let's take a look at the Microsoft accessories available for the Xbox 360.

Wireless controller
Price: $49.99

While each Xbox 360 configuration comes with a wireless controller, if you plan to play cooperatively or head-to-head with someone in the same room, you're going to need another controller (or three) to make it possible. The Wireless Xbox 360 Controller uses a 2.4 GHz wireless signal and comes with a whopping 30-foot range. Of course, every controller has built-in vibration and an expansion port for adding a headset.

Custom wireless controllers

While the basic wireless controller works just fine, what you may *really* need is a custom controllers, such as a Halo 3 limited edition wireless controller (available in two varieties) or a pink, blue, and black controller. These are a lot of fun if you want your very own special controller.

Wireless racing wheel

Price $129.99

The wireless racing wheel is pretty much a must for those gamers who love racing games. With a full-sized driving wheel and two-pedal floor set, the wireless racing wheel is a fantastic way to enjoy racing games on the 360. Once you get used to it, you won't ever want to go back to a regular controller, trust me.

Wireless headset

Price: $59.99

You like to play on Xbox Live and you enjoy the interaction with gamers the world over via your headset, but the wire is driving you nuts. What do you do? You go out and get a wireless headset that works just like the wired one except it's much smaller: It fits just over your ear and includes a small microphone that's not in front of your face. It's a handy way to play on Xbox Live without having to disconnect when you walk the 20 feet to the bathroom.

Halo 3 wireless headset

Microsoft also has a headset that matches the Halo 3 edition of the Xbox 360 console. If you're a Halo 3 nut, then you may want to get this headset instead of the standard wireless headset.

Wireless networking adapter

Price: $99.99

This simple adapter allows your Xbox 360 to connect to a wireless network inside your home or business. You probably don't always have Category 5 Ethernet cable running directly to every spot you want to put your 360, so why not go wireless and use this to connect to the Internet? Setting up is a breeze, and the reliability is fantastic. For those who want to ditch the cables, this is a must-have device.

note The ubiquitous Ethernet cable that we're used to plugging in to our computers, cable modems, and routers is officially called Category 5 cable (or Cat 5).

Xbox 360 headset
Price: $19.99

This is the standard wired headset that comes with the Xbox Live kit as well as in a couple of the Xbox 360 console bundles. It connects to the expansion port of the controller and sits on your head fairly unobtrusively. The one downside to this headset is that you are physically connected to your controller (and possibly the Xbox 360), which means that if you get up from your seat you have to take the headset off and then put it on (and adjust it) when you return. Personally, this is a pretty minor stuff, and I can handle the two seconds it takes me to make the adjustment.

Faceplates
Price: $14.99

Microsoft has several special faceplates that alter the look of your 360. A faceplate is simply a piece of dressed-up plastic that snaps directly over the front of your 360 unit, thereby giving a new look to your machine. These are pure vanity, buy if your 360 is sitting out in a prominent place, then you may want to dress up your 360 a little to give it some flavor.

Memory unit (64 MB)
Price: $39.99

This flash memory unit is made and sanctioned by Microsoft. Slip the 64 MB unit in to one of the front Xbox 360 memory card slots, and use it to save games and other information.

Memory unit (512 MB)
Price: $49.99

This unit is also made and sanctioned by Microsoft, and obviously, at just $10 more than the 64 MB unit, it makes a heck of a lot more sense to purchase this one!

Hard drive (20 GB)
Price: $99.99

The 20-GB Xbox 360 Hard Drive is intended for those
Arcade systems that didn't come with a hard drive to
begin with. There's no reason to purchase this unless
your original hard drive failed or was lost or you have
an Arcade system and want a hard drive so that
you can play older Xbox games. Truth is, the 120 GB
version is a much better value.

Hard drive (120 GB)
Price: $179.99

If you are looking to upgrade the hard drive on your
360, then this is definitely the way to do it because
dollar for dollar it's the best value. 120 GB of storage
gives you plenty of room to store pictures, movies,
game demos, videos, and whatever else you want on
your Xbox 360.

HD DVD player

Price: $179.99

This is a great addition if you're into high-definition content. The sole purpose of this DVD player is to play HD DVDs on your 360 in splendid high definition on your television or monitor. The quality is outstanding, and it's well worth the cost. I have one, and watching movies such as *King Kong* and *Mission Impossible III* in high definition is amazing.

Universal remote

Price: $39.99

The Universal Remote is a handy unit designed for those who use their 360 as a media center (for example, watching DVDs on their 360). This controller allows you to play DVDs, manage music, scroll through photos, and even control your television and stereo all from a single remote. For those who are using their 360 as a media center, this is a must.

Component AV cable
Price: $39.99

Component AV cables are necessary for high definition viewing of both HD DVD movies and Xbox 360
games. The only other way to get HD content to
your television or monitor is through an HDMI cable,
which comes standard with the Xbox 360 Elite.

Quick Charge Kit
Price: $29.99

The Xbox wireless controllers require power, and
while you can run your controllers off AA batteries,
perhaps a more efficient and easier way to manage
their power is with the power packs and the Quick
Charge Kit, which charges those packs up for you
and lets you swap in fully charged packs when the
current packs are exhausted.

Messenger Kit
Price: $29.99

The Messenger Kit is
a great little device
that includes a chat
pad and connects to
the expansion port
on your controller. You
can use this device's
QWERTY keyboard to quickly and easily communicate with others or enter data (such as addresses or
credit card numbers) into the 360. The chat pad is
also backlit, so you can clearly see the letters you are
punching even in the darkest of settings.

Xbox Live Vision (camera)

Price: $39.99

This tiny USB camera gives you the ability (via Xbox Live) to video chat with folks directly. It also works with such games as World Championship Poker where all the players have cameras trained on their mugs so that they can't hide on the Internet. Now you won't be able to keep to yourself your poker face!

Third-Party Accessories

The Xbox has hundreds of third-party accessories, and frankly, it's both impractical and impossible to list them all here. Rather than offer an exhaustive list, I'll cover the most auspicious of the accessories, so you know what's out there and what might be of use to you.

Mad Catz NFL controllers

Price: $39.99
Manufacturer: Mad Catz

These are basically wired Xbox 360 controllers decked out in the colors of your favorite NFL team. Presumably, you're playing a lot of Madden NFL 08, so it makes sense to own a functional controller that shows your team spirit.

Charge Station

Price: $34.99
Manufacturer: Nyko

This two-slot charge station allows you to plop in discharged charge packs from wireless controllers and recharge them up quickly. It's a less-expensive alternative to the Microsoft recharger.

Air Cooler

Price: $19.99
Manufacturer: Intec

This cooling system
for the Xbox 360
moves a heck of a
lot more air through
the 360 than would
otherwise flow
through. This is a
good idea since some

360s have reportedly died from over-heating problems. It's powered by its own AC adapter.

Ear Force X3 wireless headphones

Price: $99.99
Manufacturer: Turtle Beach

These high-end wireless headphones
fit over your ears and are made for
comfort and to isolate you from
the outside world. For those who
really love to be in the moment
and enjoy the best
quality, these
may be the answer.

Xbox 360 Harmony remote

Price: $99.99
Manufacturer: Logitech

Logitech designed its high-end remote control specifically to integrate the Xbox 360 into your home theatre system. If you're looking for an all-in-one remote control to manage everything *including* your Xbox 360 and Media Center applications, then this may be your best choice.

MC2 racing wheel

Price: $69.99
Manufacturer: Mad Catz

From Mad Catz, this racing wheel includes vibration feedback, rubber grips, suction cups to mount the wheel on a table, ten buttons on the wheel, and a stick shift on the controller itself. For racing enthusiasts, this isn't a bad unit to take a look at if you're not interested in the Microsoft wireless racing wheel.

Xbox 360 Gamers Screen

Price: $199.99
Manufacturer: Intec

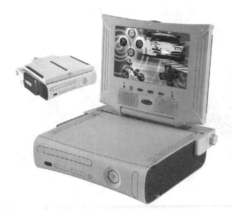

Ever wish that the Xbox 360 could be played anywhere that there was power? Ever wish that you didn't have to be near a television to play? Well, my friends, your wish is Intec's command because it has created the Xbox 360 Gamers Screen, which is designed specifically to work with your Xbox 360. This unit has a 9.2-inch TFT color screen and built-in stereo speakers. It's time to get gaming on the road!

Guitar Hero wireless controller

Price: $59.99
Manufacturer: RedOctane

This guitar controller is for the hit game Guitar Hero I, II, (and now) III. Just like real guitar heroes onstage, a wire can cramp your style, so if you find yourself playing a lot of Guitar Hero and the cord is harshing your mellow, this is the way to Guitar Hero nirvana (the place; not the band).

8

The 360 As a Media Center

Most people think of the Xbox 360 purely as a gaming console, but it can also serve as a multimedia machine and the centerpiece of your home theater and stereo system. While the Xbox 360 contains a functional DVD player—and with an HD AV cable you can enjoy games in high definition and DVD movies in 480p—with the addition of a $179.99 HD DVD player you can watch HD DVDs on your Xbox 360.

This chapter takes a look at the Xbox 360's role as a partial or complete member of your home media center. Whether you're prepared to go all-out and purchase Windows Media Center or not, you can use the Xbox 360 as your home entertainment system without too much niggling to get it up and running.

The Xbox As a DVD Player

The Xbox works as a DVD player right out of the box, able to play standard DVDs. While normal DVDs aren't high definition, you can set the Xbox 360 to output its signal in 480p so that the DVD signal is as crisp and as stable as possible (**Figure 8.1**). To set up 480p output simply go to the Xbox Dashboard's System tab and then select Console Settings and then Display; once you're at this area you can see the option to select HDTV output. For detailed instructions on how to set this on your Xbox 360, check out the instructions in Chapter 2 under "Video Display Connections."

Figure 8.1
Set your HD TV to display at 480p so that you can take advantage of extracrisp DVD settings.

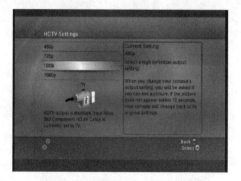

note If you want to enjoy 480p, 720p, 1080i or 1080p high-definition television output, then you're going to need an HDTV-ready television. Fortunately, many new televisions for sale now have this capability.

You can set your output to 480p even if you don't have HD DVD discs so that you can enjoy at least some of the nice benefits of a pseudo high-definition picture without the cost of a true high-definition box.

HD DVD vs. Blu-ray

A few years ago, companies started looking at the next generation of DVD media and players. This next generation, so the thinking went, should be able to show entire movies in a high-definition format with plenty of enhanced features, such as multiple angles and storyboards that can be dropped into a picture-in-picture display during movie playback.

Similar to what happened with the competing formats of Sony Betamax and VHS, the main players in the industry can't agree on a single format so they have come up with two incompatible formats: Toshiba and HD DVD on one side and Sony and its Blu-ray on the other. Right now, a big difference between Blu-ray and HD DVD is the amount of information that each disc can contain: A Blue-ray disc can hold 50 GB, and an HD DVD can hold 30 GB. (For comparison, a DVD disc can hold about 4.7 GB of information.) Each side has it strong backers, especially in the game consoles: Sony's PlayStation 3 comes with a Blue-ray drive and Microsoft's Xbox offers an HD DVD drive. Which format is going to win? Who knows, but Blu-ray looks to have the technological advantage. That said, Betamax was better than VHS, and we know what happened to that! (it died.)

HD DVD

If you are serious about watching movies on your Xbox 360 and the highest of quality is important to you, then you should probably go get yourself the HD DVD drive (**FIGURE 8.2**) from Microsoft (See Chapter 7, "Xbox Accessories"). The $179.99 Xbox 360 HD DVD Player is relatively inexpensive and gives you a stand-alone DVD drive for movies; this then means that you can use the HD DVD drive strictly for DVD and HD DVD movies and save the primary drive on the Xbox 360 for Xbox 360 or Xbox games. Select which drive you want to use in the Xbox Live menu, so if you want to watch a movie, you select the movie, and if you want to play a game, select the game.

Figure 8.2
The Xbox 360
HD DVD drive
facing front.

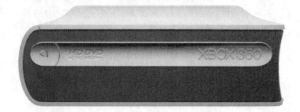

The Effect of the PlayStation 2

Back in the misty days when the PlayStation 2 was first hitting the market, the world was in the midst of small media revolution: The shift from VHS video tapes to the then-relatively new technology of DVD. At the time, however, DVD players were running upward of a thousand bucks each, and while viewers loved the crystal-clear picture and fabulous feature set of DVDs, most folks weren't prepared to shell out a grand for such luxury. Enter the PlayStation 2 machine from Sony, which was priced to get as many of them into the marketplace as possible. What made the PlayStation 2 special was that the drive on it was, in fact, a fully functional DVD player and the PS2 could play DVD movies!

Needless to say, the $399 price tag of the PS2 made it highly attractive because it give the purchaser a state-of-the-art video game console *and* a DVD player at less than half the cost of a stand-alone DVD drive. This move by Sony turned out to be sheer genius, and the PS2 ended up selling millions of units worldwide, becoming the de facto king of video game consoles.

The results of Sony's move with the PS2 and the DVD player can be seen today with the Xbox 360. The 360 contains many great multimedia improvements, such as 1080p high-definition output and connectivity to home computers for sharing music and photo files. Ultimately, however, the really nice feature of the Xbox 360 is that you can purchase an external Xbox 360 HD DVD Player for $179.99 (which is a heck of a lot cheaper than the current price of other stand-alone HD DVD players).

The 360 As a Picture Viewer

One of the great things about the 360 is that it is capable of storing vast amounts of pictures on its hard drive. You can use these pictures for anything from wallpaper to screensavers to slide shows for family members, but no matter how you decide to use your photos on the 360, you need to know how to access them and put them to use.

Figure 8.3
The Media area is where you find the Pictures tab.

From the Media page in the Xbox 360 Dashboard, select Pictures (**Figure 8.3**) to see which photos you have on your 360. Once you are in this page, you have four categories of photos waiting: Computer, Digital Camera, Current Disc, and Portable Device. Let's take a look at what each of these actually represents (**Figure 8.4**).

Figure 8.4

If you have everything connected, you can have all four picture categories (Computer, Digital Camera, Current Disc, and Portable Device) active at once.

Computer

The Computer selection shows the current computer or computers connected to your Xbox 360 through either a local wired or a wireless network. To connect to a Windows-based computer you need only select the computer and press the A button (on your 360's controller) to attach to it. If you are having connection troubles you can test the connection (**Figure 8.5**) to see if there are any problems.

Figure 8.5

You may have to test the connection to your PC if you're having problems getting hooked up.

Once connected to your Windows PC, you can stream whatever media you have made available from the PC. To get shared media off of the PC, you need to be running Windows Media Center or Windows Media Player 11. Windows Media Player, or WMP, is the more ubiquitous program, and since it's free, I'll concentrate on it here.

In WMP 11, you can set the sharing properties of your PC-based media by clicking the Library menu and then selecting Sharing. This brings up a sharing window (**Figure 8.6**) where you can select the Xbox on the current network that you'd like to share your media with and which media you specifically want to share.

Figure 8.6
You have to tell your PC to share media with your Xbox, and that's done in Windows Media Player 11 by selection Sharing from the Library menu.

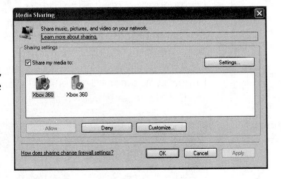

Digital Camera

You can connect your digital camera directly to the Xbox 360's USB port. When you turn the camera on, the 360 automatically recognizes it (in this case, a Cannon EOS Rebel XTi) and shows you a panel of the photos available for viewing (**Figure 8.7**). You can either play a slide show directly from the camera or you can select individual pictures to view or to set as a background image. While you can't upload shots from your camera to your 360 through this screen, you can put your photos on a CD and have it sitting in your drive ready to go at any time.

Figure 8.7
Connect your camera to the 360's USB port to get the camera up and running.

Viewing Slide Shows

If you want to view a slide show, you just need to select the Play Slideshow button. However, once the slide show is underway, you may want to pause or move forward through particular shots or alter them a little. If this is your desire, just hit the control stick on your controller during the slide show and a control panel pops up (**FIGURE 8.8**), which gives you the option of moving forward or back, stopping, shuffling the shots, or even rotating the shots right or left.

Figure 8.8
A small control panel comes on screen if you tap your control stick during photo playback.

Current Disc

If you have a CD or DVD with your own photos stored on it, you can place the disc in the 360's disc tray and it shows up immediately as the Current Disc in the picture area (**FIGURE 8.9**). By selecting the images on the disc, you can play a slide show or set them as background images just like any other images you have access to.

Figure 8.9
A photo CD or DVD placed in the Xbox 360's drive shows up immediately.

Portable Device

A portable device is basically any storage device with a USB connector. In this case, I attached a USB memory stick with photos on it to the USB port on the 360 and it showed up under the Portable Device category immediately. As usual, when you select the Portable Device, all of the pictures on your device (or the folders that contain the pictures) show up in the panel on the right (**Figure 8.10**).

Figure 8.10
A USB drive shows up as a portable device with pictures on it when plugged in to the 360.

Once the slide show gets going, you can just sit back and enjoy it (**FIGURE 8.11**) from the comfort of your chair. You can use the Xbox wireless (or wired) controllers or a universal remote to control the show.

Figure 8.11
Once the slides get rolling, you can sit back and enjoy the show.

The 360 As an Audio Player

You can also use your 360 as a jukebox of digital music. This is especially easy to do if you have a Microsoft Zune or are using Windows Media Player 11 or Windows Media Center on a connected PC. If this is the case, you can use these packages to route the music through your 360. The Zune software (**FIGURE 8.12**) is set up specifically to connect to an Xbox 360.

Figure 8.12
The Zune software is ready and waiting for an Xbox 360 that's connected to your PC.

The Music access point for the 360 is also in the Media menu, which you access by simply selecting the Music tab. Once you do this, you are given a list of possible devices that might hold music (**Figure 8.13**).

Figure 8.13
You have five main methods of music connection to the 360.

If you read the section earlier in this chapter about how to work with photos, this will seem very familiar: You can access songs through a PC or you can find them directly on the 360 via a CD, DVD, or a device attached by a USB cable. The connection options are as follows:

- **Music Player.** The most obvious of these is, of course, the Microsoft Zune player, but if the Zune is not one of the players you own, the 360 is capable of "noticing" quite a few other MP3 players on the market.

- **Hard Drive.** Obviously, the hard drive on the Xbox 360 is a solid place to find music files. You may have purchased some of these files with Microsoft Points from the Xbox Live Marketplace and some of them may have come from the Zune Marketplace, but either way, the 360's hard drive is often a reservoir for files.

- **Computer.** If your computer is connected to the same network as the 360 and you've allowed sharing of files, you can stream music directly from your PC to the 360 for playback.

- **Current Disc.** If you have a music CD in the 360, you can play the songs through your 360.

- **Portable Device.** Any USB flash drive or USB hard-disk drive with music files shows up under this category when you attach it to the Xbox 360.

The Xbox 360 As a Video Player

The 360 can play video spectacularly in high definition. As mentioned in Chapter 6, "Shopping with the Xbox 360," the Xbox Live Marketplace offers all kinds of free videos, and once you've downloaded them to your 360's hard drive, they're ready to rock and/or roll. When you select the Video tab from the Media window (**Figure 8.14**) you are taken to an area that gives you four choices: Console (the hard drive of your 360), Computer (a Windows-based PC connected to the same network as your 360), Current Disc (a disc that's in your 360's drive), and Portable Device (an external flash or hard-disk drive with video content on it).

Figure 8.14
The Video tab in the Media window takes you here.

Console (hard-drive) videos

The highest-quality videos are usually those you download from the Xbox Live area; you will find these stored on the Console area (the hard drive of your 360). Selecting this area takes you to a list of the videos, which are broken down by category (**Figure 8.15**).

Figure 8.15
The HD videos shown here were all downloaded from Xbox Live.

When watching the video you've selected, hitting the control stick in any direction brings up the small control panel (**Figure 8.16**) that gives you the ability to control the video playback and displays an information panel about the video itself.

Figure 8.16
Once you're watching a video, you can pull up a panel to control the playback.

Windows Media Center

Windows Media Center is a special home entertainment application that's designed to act as an all-in-one hub for the user's videos, music, pictures, games, and other entertainment information. Windows Media Center (WMC) is available as a stand-alone application and is part of the Windows Vista Home Premium and Ultimate editions.

WMC comes with a special remote control that allows the user to access all of the entertainment information on their PC at once. And with a program called Windows Media Center Extender, the full functionality of Windows Media Center can be extended to the Xbox 360, thereby allowing the user to do a handful of media-related activities including:

- Watching television.

- Listening to music.

- Watching commercial videos.

- Watching home videos.

- Viewing photographs.

- Listening to radio (including Internet radio).

- Watching Internet TV.

- Controlling portable media devices such as the Zune.

- Streaming video and audio to other PCs and locations such as stereos with Wi-Fi receivers on a network.

A

Microsoft's Official List of
Backward-Compatible Xbox Games

The Xbox team is working to let gamers play original Xbox games on the Xbox 360. (To play Xbox games on your Xbox 360 console, you need a hard disk drive.)

The number of games is constantly growing, but as we go to press with this book, here is the official list of backward-compatible games.

4x4 EVO 2

AirForce Delta Storm

Aggressive Inline

Alias

Aliens versus Predator Extinction

All-Star Baseball 2003

All-Star Baseball 2005

America's Army: Rise of a Soldier

Amped: Freestyle Snowboarding

Amped 2

Aquaman: Battle of Atlantis

Army Men: Sarge's War

Atari Anthology

ATV: Quad Power Racing 2

Auto Modellista

Avatar: The Last Airbender

Bad Boys 2

Bass Pro Shops Trophy Hunter 2007

Big Mutha Truckers

Baldur's Gate: Dark Alliance II

Barbarian

Barbie Horse Adventures Wild Horse Rescue

Batman Begins

Battle Engine Aquila

Battlestar Galactica

Black

Blinx 2 : Masters of Time & Space

BloodRayne 2

BMX XXX

Breakdown

Brute Force

Buffy the Vampire Slayer

Buffy the Vampire Slayer: Chaos Bleeds

Burnout

Burnout 3: Takedown

Cabela's Big Game Hunter 2005 Adventures

Cabela's Dangerous Hunts

Cabela's Outdoor Adventures 06

Cabela's Deer Hunt 2004 Season

Cabela's Deer Hunt 2005 Season

Call of Cthulhu: Dark Corners of the Earth

Call of Duty: Finest Hour

Call of Duty 2: Big Red One

Call of Duty 3

Cars

Casino

Catwoman

Chicago Enforcer

Circus Maximus

Close Combat: First to Fight

Colin McRae Rally 4

Combat Elite: WWII Paratroopers

Commandos 2: Men of Courage

Conflict: Desert Storm

Conker: Live and Reloaded

Constantine

Counter-Strike

Crash Bandicoot 4

Crash Bandicoot 5: Wrath of Cortex

Crash Twinsanity

Crash Nitro Kart 2

Crimson Skies: High Road to Revenge

Crouching Tiger, Hidden Dragon

Dai Senryaku VII: Modern Military Tactics

Dark Angel

Darkwatch

The Da Vinci Code

Dead or Alive 3

Dead Or Alive Ultimate

Dead to Rights

Deathrow

Destroy All Humans!

Digimon Rumble Arena 2

Dinotopia2

Doom 3

Doom 3: Resurrection of Evil

Drake

Dreamfall: The Longest Journey

Drive to Survive

Dynasty Warriors 4

Egg Mania: Eggstreme Madness

The Elder Scrolls III: Morrowind

ESPN College Hoops

ESPN Major League Baseball

ESPN MLS ExtraTime 2002

ESPN NHL 2K5

Euro 2004

Evil Dead: A Fistful of Boomstick

Evil Dead: Regeneration

Ex-Chaser

F1 2001

Family Guy

Fable

Fable: The Lost Chapters

Fairly Odd Parents: Breakin' da Rules

Far Cry: Instincts

Fatal Frame

Fatal Frame II: Crimson Butterfly Director's Cut

FIFA Soccer 2003

FIFA Soccer 2004

FIFA Soccer 2007

FIFA Street

FIFA Street 2

Fight Night 2004

Flatout

Ford Mustang

Ford vs. Chevy

Forza Motorsport

Freaky Flyers

Frogger Beyond

Full Spectrum Warrior

Full Spectrum Warrior: Ten Hammers

Futurama

Fuzion Frenzy

Gauntlet: Seven Sorrows

Genma Onimusha

Goblin Commander: Unleash the Horde

Grabbed by the Ghoulies

Grand Theft Auto: San Andreas

Grand Theft Auto: The Trilogy

Grand Theft Auto: Vice City

Gravity Games Bike: Street. Vert. Dirt.

The Great Escape

Grooverider: Slot Car Thunder

Guilty Gear Isuka

Guilty Gear X2 #Reload

Half-Life 2

Halo

Halo 2

Halo 2 Multiplayer Map Pack

Harry Potter and the Chamber of Secrets

Harry Potter and the Goblet of Fire

Harry Potter and the Prisoner of Azkaban

Harry Potter and the Sorcerer's Stone

He-Man: Defender of Grayskull

Hitman: Contracts

Hot Wheels: Stunt Track Challenge

House of the Dead 3

The Hulk

I-Ninja

The Incredible Hulk: Ultimate Destruction

The Incredibles: Rise of the Underminer

IHRA Drag Racing Sportsman Edition

IHRA Professional Drag Racing 2005

Indigo Prophecy

Incredibles

IndyCar Series 2005

Intellivision Lives

Jade Empire3

James Bond 007: NightFire

JSRF: Jet Set Radio Future

Judge Dredd: Dredd vs. Death

Jurassic Park: Operation Genesis

Justice League Heroes

Kabuki Warriors

Kelly Slater's Pro Surfer

kill.switch

King Arthur

The King of Fighters 2002 & 2003

The King of Fighters Neowave

Kingdom Under Fire: The Crusaders

The Legend of Spyro: A New Beginning

Leisure Suit Larry: Magna Cum Laude

Legends of Wrestling

Lego Star Wars

Lego Star Wars II: The Original Trilogy

Lemony Snicket's A Series of Unfortunate Events

Links 2004

Loons—The Fight for Fame

The Lord of the Rings: The Return of the King

Magatama

Magic: The Gathering—Battleground

Manhunt

Marvel Nemesis: Rise of the Imperfects

Marvel vs. Capcom 2

Mat Hoffman's Pro BMX 2

Max Payne

Max Payne 2

Maximum Chase

MechAssault 2: Lone Wolf

Medal of Honor European Assault

Medal of Honor Frontline

Medal of Honor Rising Sun

Mega Man Anniversary Collection

Mercenaries

Metal Arms: Glitch in the System

MicroMachines

Mike Tyson Heavyweight Boxing

Minority Report

MLB SlugFest 20-03

MLB SlugFest 20-04

Monster Garage

Mortal Kombat: Armageddon

Mortal Kombat Deception

MotoGP

MotoGP 2

MTV Music Generator 3

MTX: Mototrax

Murakumo: Renegade Mech Pursuit

MX Unleashed

MX vs. ATV Unleashed

MX World Tour: Featuring Jamie Little

Myst III: Exile

Namco Museum

Namco Museum 50th Anniversary Arcade Collection

NASCAR 2006: Total Team Control

NBA Live 2002

NBA LIVE 2004

NCAA Football 06

Need For Speed Underground 2

NFL Blitz 2002

NFL Blitz 2003

NFL Blitz 2004

NFL Fever 2004

NHL 2004

NHL Hitz 2003

Ninja Gaiden

Ninja Gaiden Black

Oddworld: Munch's Oddysee

Open Season

Outlaw Golf 2

Outlaw Golf: 9 More Holes of X-mas

Outlaw Tennis

Outlaw Volleyball

Outlaw Volleyball: Red Hot

OutRun 2

OutRun 2006: Coast to Coast

Over the Hedge

Pac-Man World 3

Pariah

Panzer Dragoon Orta

Phantom Crash

Phantom Dust

Pinball Hall of Fame

Pitfall: The Lost Expedition

Predator Concrete Jungle

Prince of Persia: The Sands of Time

Pro Evolution Soccer 5

Pro Race Driver

Project Gotham Racing

Project Gotham Racing 2

Psychonauts

Pump It Up: Exceed

The Punisher

Pure Pinball

Puyo Pop Fever2

Quantum Redshift

RalliSport Challenge

Rainbow Six Lockdown

Rapala Pro Fishing

Rayman Arena

Raze's Hell

Red Dead Revolver

Red Faction II

RedCard 2003

Reservoir Dogs

Return to Castle Wolfenstein

Richard Burns Rally

RoadKill

Robotech: Battlecry

Rocky Legends

Rogue Ops

Rogue Trooper

Rugby League 2

Samurai Jack

Samurai Warriors

Scarface

Scooby Doo! Night of 100 Frights

Scrapland

Sega GT 2002

Sega GT Online

Serious Sam

Shadow The Hedgehog

Shadow Ops: Red Mercury

Shamu's Deep Sea Adventures

Shark Tale

ShellShock: Nam '67

Shenmue II

Shincho Mahjong

Sid Meier's Pirates!

The Simpsons Hit and Run

The Simpsons Road Rage

Sims 2

Silent Hill 2: Restless Dreams

Silent Hill 4: The Room

Smashing Drive

Sneakers 5

Sniper Elite

Soccer Slam

Sonic Heroes

Sonic Mega Collection Plus

Sonic Riders

Soul Calibur 2

Spawn Armageddon

Speed Kings

Sphinx and the Cursed Mummy

Spider-Man

Spider-Man 2

Splat Magazine Renegade Paintball

Splinter Cell: Double Agent

SpongeBob SquarePants: Battle for Bikini Bottom

SpongeBob SquarePants: Lights, Camera, Pants!

The SpongeBob SquarePants Movie

SpyHunter 2

SpyHunter: Nowhere to Run

Spyro A Hero's Tail

SSX 3

Stake

Star Wars Battlefront

Star Wars Battlefront II

Star Wars: Episode III Revenge of the Sith

Star Wars Jedi Knight: Jedi Academy

Star Wars: Knights of the Old Republic

Star Wars Knights of the Old Republic II: The Sith Lords

Star Wars Republic Commando

State of Emergency

Street Fighter Anniversary Collection

Street Racing Syndicate

Stubbs the Zombie in Rebel without a Pulse

The Suffering

Super Bubble Pop

Super Monkey Ball Deluxe

SX Superstar

Taz Wanted

Tecmo Classic Arcade

Teenage Mutant Ninja Turtles

The Terminator Dawn of Fate

Test Drive: Eve of Destruction

Tetris Worlds4

The Thing

Thief: Deadly Shadows

Tiger Woods PGA Tour 07

TMNT Mutant Melee

Tom Clancy's Ghost Recon

Tom Clancy's Ghost Recon 2

Tom Clancy's Ghost Recon: Island Thunder

Tom Clancy's Ghost Recon 2 Summit Strike

Tom Clancy's Rainbow Six 3

Tom Clancy's Rainbow Six 3 Black Arrow

Tom Clancy's Splinter Cell

Tom Clancy's Splinter Cell Chaos Theory

Tom Clancy's Splinter Cell Double Agent

Tom Clancy's Splinter Cell Pandora Tomorrow

Tony Hawk's American Wasteland

Tony Hawk's Pro Skater 2x

Tony Hawk's Pro Skater 3

Tony Hawk's Pro Skater 4

Tony Hawk's Underground

Tony Hawk's Underground 2

Torino 2006 Winter Olympics

Tork: Prehistoric Punk

Toxic Grind

Transworld Surf

Trigger Man

Trivial Pursuit Unhinged

True Crime: Streets of LA

Ty The Tasmanian Tiger

Ty the Tasmanian Tiger 2: Bush Rescue

Ty the Tasmanian Tiger 3: Night of the Quinkan

Ultimate Spider-Man

Ultra Bust-A-Move

Unreal Championship 2: The Liandri Conflict

Urban Freestyle Soccer

The Urbz: Sims In The City

Vexx

Vietcong: Purple Haze

Volvo: Drive for Life

Wakeboarding Unleashed: Featuring Sean Murray

Whacked!

Winback 2: Project Poseidon

Without Warning

World Soccer Winning Eleven 8 International

World Soccer Winning Eleven 9

World Series Baseball 2K3

Worms 4 Mayhem

Worms Forts: Under Siege

Wrath Unleashed

WWE Raw

WWE Raw 2

X2 Wolverine's Revenge

Xiaolin Showdown

XIII

Yourself!Fitness

Yu-Gi-Oh! The Dawn of Destiny

Zapper

B

Xbox Resources

As you would expect, you can find a vibrant Xbox 360 community on the Web. Here are some of the best sources of information on the Xbox 360 console and games.

BoxCheats
www.boxcheats.com
A good spot for cheats.

Console Cheat Codes
www.consolecheatcodes.com
Another good spot for cheats.

GameFAQ
www.gamefaqs.com
Find online strategy here.

GameSpot
www.gamespot.com
Check here for game reviews.

GameSpy
http://xbox360.gamespy.com
Useful information about
online gaming.

GameZone
http://xbox360.gamezone.com
Handy news, reviews, inter-
views, and articles.

IGN Entertainment
www.ign.com
Look here for game reviews.

TeamXbox
www.teamxbox.com
Lots of Xbox news and reviews.

Xbox 360 Cheats
www.xbox360cheats.com
A good clearinghouse for
cheats.

Xbox365
www.xbox365.com
Check here for cheats, reviews,
and more.

Xbox official site
www.xbox.com
The first place you should go
for forums, cheats, games, and
so on.

Xbox Today
www.xboxtoday.ca
Specializes in Xbox news and
rumors.

Index